Unseen Path

Linda H. Williams

BLUE INK
PRESS

I have tried to recreate events, locales and conversations from my memories of them. In order to maintain their anonymity in some instances I have changed the names of individuals and places, I may have changed some identifying characteristics and details such as physical properties, occupations and places of residence.

Published by Blue Ink Press, LLC

Printed in the United States of America

Cover design by Shari Ryan

www.blueinkpress.com

ISBN: 0-9968673-1-7
ISBN-13: 978-0-9968673-1-3
Library of Congress Control Number: 2016948065

I dedicate this book to my family—some born into this family and some grafted in, but all carry a piece that makes us family. You are brave to daily walk our path, and I thank you for your unconditional love freely given to me. To Sam, the head of this family, you are my forever HERO!

CONTENTS

FOREWORD

As I sit in the gym of Athens Drive High School watching my daughter dance around and spin her flag with the other members of the winter guard, I wonder how this life we are living will shape her into the adult she will be one day. Until now, I have not given much thought about how God's calling on our lives will affect our children in their adulthood. As a mom with my own family, I look back at my childhood from a different perspective and see that our experiences were not always typical. As a child, I never had the thought that my family or our life was different from anyone else. Truthfully, we all have a different definition of normal and our own unique journey. I have had the privilege of reading this book that not only documents events, but also connects the dots for me on how God has spoken His truth to our family. I can now see the lessons we have learned along the way. I realize that much of how I think about things and process situations is a result of all God has taught my family. The biggest gift that my parents gave me is the faith to see that God works ALL things for our good. I hope that I have done a good job of passing that faith on to my five children.

— *Tara Flowers, oldest daughter of Linda H. Williams*

When I was growing up, I had no clue my family was different from other families. I knew I was happy, loved, and safe and that was all that mattered. It wasn't until I became an adult that I realized the impact my family had on my life. It is fascinating being able to connect the dots between my family's story and the path God is leading me on as a wife and mother. I'm able to refuse to be afraid of the unknown future, I'm able to trust God when He asks me to do things that are hard or illogical. I am confident, even when life gets painful and rocky, that God is in control and using everything for my good and His glory.

— *Leah Bowman, youngest daughter of Linda H. Williams*

i

Chapter 1
With Love From Jesus

Come, let us tell of the LORD's greatness; let us exalt his name together.
Psalm 34:3, NLT

The dock door is raised. The lights come on. Footsteps are heard coming up the steps. The sound of praise music is playing faintly in the background. An old pickup truck pulls into the loading dock. A dusty and dated warehouse building on the back side of an often forgotten shopping center in southeast Raleigh comes to life for yet another day. Volunteers begin unloading the truck of its precious cargo of bread, desserts, and other goodies gleaned from a local merchant. Laughter and hugs invade the space. Tears and prayers are shared. A new day has begun at With Love From Jesus Ministries (WLFJ).

Four days each week, those in the community with great physical, spiritual, and emotional needs arrive to discover the treasures that Jesus has left for them in this building. Single moms, the elderly, the disabled, the discouraged, broken fami-

1

lies, the jobless, the homeless, the forgotten, the overlooked, the sick, illegal immigrants, English speaking, Spanish speaking, black, white, Asian, Muslim, the rejected, the abused, the neglected, alcoholics and more—these are our honored guests. Hundreds come each week and are served by some of the more than 200 people who volunteer over the course of a month. Each person is welcomed by one of these sweet servants of the King of Glory, invited to hear a short Bible message, offered prayer, given a shopping cart, and shown the love of Christ as they receive needed resources for their struggling family. Some will choose to stop in the prayer center to receive prayers, hugs, Bibles, and the name of a church for follow-up, but all in attendance will be blessed with goodies for their families. Shopping carts are filled with clothing, shoes, household items (such as linens, dishes, paper products, etc.), bread, produce, sweet treats, non-perishable foods and deli/meat items. While some will enter into a relationship with Jesus or experience healing or freedom from addiction, all will be blessed and encouraged.

Even though many needs are met, many prayers offered in the name of Jesus, and many people encouraged, this is not the reason With Love From Jesus exists. This ministry was designed by God to be a platform to display the unity of the Body of Christ. The real focus, the real ministry, the real excitement is seen as Believers in Jesus from all walks of life and denominational backgrounds come together to demonstrate their love for Jesus by loving each other and serving together. They display to these honored guests that we are One.

At the end of Acts 2, we read that the Church was focused and moving in a united purpose. The result of this display of unity was that needs were being met and people were being saved. These early disciples did not set out to see how many people they could get to receive Christ or how many people they could feed; they were simply living the united life. The results were amazing!

Sixteen years ago, during the early days of WLFJ, we were all about meeting human needs as we sought daily to reveal the love of Christ to our neighbors. A local grocery store told the pastor of our small church that they were throwing away hundreds of dollars of good food every day and asked if there was a way our church could take the food and use it to help people in the community. The opportunity presented itself. Our church agreed to give it a try. We made up bags of food daily and packed into cars to share with our community. Two garages were set up as work stations. Six days a week, bags were packed and church members hit the streets looking for those who needed help.

The church was very small because it had gone through a painful split and most of the members had scattered to other places. Sin invaded what had been a growing and dynamic church family and left only three families, including ours, in leadership. God's instruction to the families left was to stay together and not to dissolve the church. All three families were in a ministry that was once supported by a church that was no more, and now they found themselves in their own places of great need. With the food from the local grocery store, those of us in ministry were fed, and the remainder of the food was bagged and given away as quickly as possible, as the next day would bring more.

As weeks turned into months, our small group became stretched too thin with the demands of this new and growing ministry. It was time to look for help. We invited other small churches to get involved. A third garage became another work station. A sister grocery store to the one donating called and asked if they too could have their extra food picked up to help serve needs in the community. The ministry was growing by leaps and bounds. Workers seemed too few to meet the growing needs. As it became apparent that this ministry was greater than any one church, we invited other churches to join the outreach, but many were hesitant to join with another church's ministry. Somehow this work needed to be separated from our little church so it could stand on its own. Nonprofit status was our next step, and eighteen months after beginning, WLFJ became a 501c3. Six months later, the ministry moved into its first warehouse space. The set up was very different from the garage stage. Now guests could make their own choices and enjoy their own "shopping" experience. (We use the term *shopping* in reference to our guests' experience receiving the donated goods.) For many, WLFJ became their local grocery store. For those of us walking through this stage, it seemed very strange. There was no advertisement of an opening and yet the crowds came. God had us on His training ground and was moving us ahead. Within 60 days we moved into a larger space.

At first we tried to be open daily, but the crowds overwhelmed our few workers. We had to get organized. Going to people with pre-made bags was very different from people coming to us and shopping. We cut back to four days a week to give ourselves some recovery and organization time. As folks came and received, we looked for every opportunity to share Jesus one-on-one, but just keeping food on the shelves seemed to be more than we could do. Before long we realized we had to make sharing Jesus intentional or it would not happen. We started seating our guests to hear a short Bible message before they started their shopping experience. After they were released to shop, another group was welcomed into the building. This would happen several times each day as folks arrived to shop.

By word of mouth, people heard about our work. Additional volunteers joined to help, and more and more guests came to receive. A few churches sent teams of volunteers or held nonperishable food drives. Vendors donated food and other resources. A whirlwind of a year went by as we learned more by our mistakes than our planning. The three families were struggling to see provision for their own families as this new and unplanned ministry continued to grow. Our lease came to an end after a year with no opportunity to renew it. Two months later, WLFJ moved into what would become its permanent location in an old shopping center in southeast Raleigh.

Though the gospel was being given, our focus was still more on meeting practical needs, with the measuring stick being how many bags of groceries were given away. God called one of the three families in leadership to move on to another place of ministry. We had to regroup and adjust our plans to this big shift in leadership and manpower. With only two families left to lead a small team of volunteers and serve nearly a hundred families a day, it was a stretching time. It was during this period that God helped us to see that our focus needed to transition from bags of groceries to giving the Word. Every day we looked for that right person to share the Word with our guests, and for volunteers to serve in all areas—which now included clothing, household items, books, and sometimes even furniture—and manage the growing needs and expenses of WLFJ.

With a $5,000 monthly lease and no revenue being generated, we initially asked the community for a small donation when they came to shop. At first we asked for one dollar, and in a short time, it was increased to three dollars. This was never a requirement to shop. No one was ever turned away. As the ministry grew, we watched this small donation cover that lease. However, when the Lord led us to be more intentional about giving the gospel, He also said to us that you don't ask the people you are evangelizing to support the work. This provision should come from the Body of Christ. This was a very difficult word to us. A few individuals and churches did give to help support the ministry; however, these gifts didn't come close to covering the lease. I met with the other board members. We labored over this decision. This small fee was how the rent was paid. Ultimately, we chose to be obedient. There would be times over the next months that I would find myself "reminding" God that He called us to take this step of faith. God has always been faithful to cover the lease.

Soon another transition came as God began to speak a new and fresh focus into this growing outreach. His reason for bringing forth this ministry was not to simply meet needs or even to share the amazing good news of Jesus. It was to be a place that rallied the Body of Christ to demonstrate to the world the beautiful unity of that Body. Often the enemy uses diversity to speak division, but God's plan is for diversity to speak completeness. The cry of our hearts was, "how do we do this, Lord Jesus?"

As the daily crowds came in to be served, WLFJ looked very much the same on the outside as it had before. Needs were met and many people received Christ, yet something was very different. Our focus had changed to enjoying the fellowship of the Family of God and serving together with joy. We didn't allow our differences to be a problem, but rather sought the one place where we could agree and serve the community. The place we agreed was very easy to find. We all agreed that there is only one way to the Father and that is through the precious blood of Jesus. So, unity is displayed!

Daily as that dock door is raised and the trucks are unloaded, shelves are stocked, and a dusty, old warehouse takes on life, the focus is now on how we can love each other well. We support each other, pray for each other, enjoy being family, and expect that the overflow from this focus will touch our community for Jesus. Yes, needs are met and the Word is richly sown into the lives of many in our community, but this is the fruit that comes from unity. Simple things—giving away food to share Jesus, unity, and family—have become the connecting dots on an unseen path in my life. When and how did I get on this path? The answer to that question goes back forty years.

Chapter 2
Getting on the Path

You have made known to me the path of life; you will fill me with joy in your presence, with eternal pleasures at your right hand.
Psalm 16:11, NIV

One of the amazing things God does when we begin our walk with Him is erase our past. All our sins and failures are wiped away by the blood of Jesus, and we begin a new life that doesn't include that debt. The other side of that blessing is also amazing. Those very things that are no longer used against us can actually be redeemed for Kingdom purposes in our new life in Christ.

Sam and I were married in 1970 and made many moves and career changes. Seven years later, and very new in Christ, we were involved in a growing business. For the first time in our lives, it seemed that we had a great future. Before Christ, we had set the huge goal of owning a distributorship. We were pushing hard toward advancement, and focusing on trying to make it big in business. Every day we would wake up with the need to push and build this business. Sam learned the warehouse end of the company as I strived to increase sales and network with people.

After taking our six-year-old daughter, Tara, to school each day, I would hit the road, traveling over several counties. In the evenings, Sam and I took turns building the business. Sam had walked away from a good job with a growing company in order for us to further this dream. However, once Jesus entered the picture, our focus changed drastically, along with our desires.

As a child my mom told me it was time to join the church. I walked down the aisle and repeated words that the preacher said, was baptized, and joined the church. Years later, when Sam and I were dating, we went to church with his aunt. An invitation was given to receive Christ. Sam went forward and I followed. We met with the pastor. We prayed together and again, I went through the motions of repeating words without any true understanding. When Tara was five years old, Sam and I decided to give church a try again. We found one near our home. I was going through a deep time of sadness after a miscarriage. We both thought going back to church would help. About a year and half later, we moved fifty miles from that home and our church. Each Sunday we felt the need to drive more than an hour to go back. Life seemed to be going well for us in some ways, but I was miserable. Confused by my mother's instructions as a child and the act of following Sam down the aisle years later, I couldn't decide whether I really knew the Lord or not! One day in desperation, I dropped to my knees beside our bed and cried out to the Lord for salvation. Everything changed after that day.

What had been a daily—and exciting—focus in business was now empty drudgery. Neither of us had any motivation or desire to keep pushing and building the company. Our eyes were opened to wrong business practices within our company. We knew we had to get out, but felt trapped. All of our finances had been invested in this business. The house we lived in, both of our jobs, and both of our vehicles were owned by the company. The lack of integrity in the business would make a lasting impression on Sam and I. Years later, when I would take the lead role at WLFJ, this memory would be a great tool that God would use to burden me for a high standard of integrity in the ministry.

Day after day we muddled through, trying to figure out what to do. Business sales dropped radically. Those in authority over us began to put great pressure on us to perform. They constantly reminded us of our goals and their investment and confidence in us. The work that had once been motivated by excitement and anticipation of a better life now became bondage and hardship. Our finances declined as the zeal for this work dissipated. During this time, I had another miscarriage. We wanted more children, but each pregnancy ended in loss. Discouragement and hopelessness became daily companions. Days turned into weeks of just getting by with no idea of what we should do.

The first time I can remember God speaking to me as a new believer was one morning soon after our realization that something needed to change with our business plans. The Lord spoke to me from Psalm 128:3: *Your wife will be like a fruitful vine within your house.* I recorded this in my journal and tried to wrap my mind around exactly what I was hearing. I shared it with Sam. As we pondered this Word together, we knew the truth. If I quit this job, Sam had to as well. We were a partnership. We struggled and didn't know what to do. We argued. We prayed. We talked. I cried! It was a very difficult time for both of us. We wanted to make the step of faith but didn't know what that looked like. We had no discipleship and were very new in the Lord and had few Christian friends. We could feel God distancing us from current friends. There was no one that we felt we could go to for advice. We were desperate before the Lord for Him to show up and help us. We were alone and wanted to cling to each other during this time, yet we were both overwhelmed by our own emotions. We erupted on each other with feelings of fear and great discouragement. There were many days when, as I forced myself to walk through the necessary tasks to keep us afloat, all I could say over and over was, "Jesus, help us."

One day, Sam and I had a huge argument. He left early on a Saturday morning and was gone all day. In our seven years of marriage, he had never just taken off without saying anything. I paced the floor all day trying to be "normal" for Tara. Tears coursed down my cheeks uncontrollably as I tried to stay busy.

The continued grief of losing another baby just weeks earlier added fuel to the pain within me. I sat by the pool in our back-yard watching Tara swim and the emptiness and vanity of all I saw around me simply added more pain. The beautiful home on huge acreage—complete with swimming pool—and the new cars parked in the garage were no comfort or help. What had once felt like paradise was now more like a prison.

The seemingly endless day was finally over when Sam re-turned. That evening he told me he had driven to Raleigh (about fifty miles from where we were living at the time) and spent all day placing applications with apartment complexes for a posi-tion as a maintenance man. He knew there would be no one there on a Saturday to talk to or acknowledge receipt of his ap-plications, but he felt like he had to do something. We prayed together and waited on the Lord. On Monday morning, one of those companies called him and hired him, sight unseen. The job came complete with an apartment. Our tears turned to laughter and excitement. We were delighted with God's provision for escape and a new life ahead. The next few weeks were spent packing and figuring out the practical steps to make this transi-tion. We moved all our things out of the spacious, beautiful house, turned in our two brand new cars, resigned from what had seemed like promising careers, and called a friend to come get us because we had no transportation. Sam bought a car, which had been parked for a year, for a hundred dollars from my brother-in-law. He pieced the car back together, and we were able to drive it for over a year as we got back on our feet. We were so very broke, but we were rich in the Lord and on the right track for the first time in our lives.

By this time, Tara was seven years old. Sam had a daughter, Lesly, from a previous marriage who lived with her mom. We loved her visits as she was with us often. We had tried many times to have other children but without success. In the weeks before our move, I sold all of our baby equipment and clothes, deciding to be thankful and content with the two daughters God had given us. We were being held by the hand of God, and we were going to be fine! Now in this place of great deliverance by

God, we found out that we were pregnant again.

Life was difficult but very exciting—a new start, another baby—yet peace reigned. The months after leaving the business were difficult financially, but also carefree. I never worried or even entertained the thought that I'd have a miscarriage. I knew our new baby was going to be full term. This baby was obviously in God's timing and part of this new stage of life for our family. Lesly and Tara were so excited about the baby. We all were excited! We settled into our new routine. Sam worked for the apartment complex and I was able to lend a little help with our finances by cleaning apartments when residents moved out. It was nearly Christmas when the doctors decided I needed an ultrasound. When they listened for a heartbeat, they heard one and then thought they heard another on the other side. At first, they thought I had twins, but the ultrasound simply showed one baby that moved very fast! The doctors moved my due date from January to before Christmas. As we rushed to make preparation for the early arrival, another twist happened that we weren't expecting. Without notice, there was a change in management and Sam lost his job. The job included our apartment. We ran to the Lord. We had seen His faithfulness in the past and knew He had not taken us this far to leave us alone. Now we had a church family and great prayer support. Within a couple of days God provided a new job for Sam in a new and beautiful apartment complex, complete with an apartment for us. This new place was spacious with plenty of room for our new baby and lots of children for Tara and Lesly to have as playmates. Our amazing church family literally picked us up and moved us in one day. Their goal was to get us in and somewhat settled, knowing that the baby could arrive at any time.

After carrying Leah weeks past my due date, she came very fast and her little body went into shock from the rapid delivery. They quickly took her from my arms and rushed her to the ICU nursery. Their initial word to us was that this was not unusual, and she would be fine. Within a few hours of her birth, the doctor came to my room to tell me that my sweet little Leah would likely not live. Sam had already picked up Tara from my mom's house and was home with her. I was alone in the hospital to handle this excruciating news. I sat in my bed and cried. I thanked the Lord for allowing me to carry this precious baby full term and for the one time I was able to hold her, and then, I gave her to Him. All I could do now was wait on the Lord. Within a few hours, the nurse came to my room to tell me that Leah had made an amazing turn and was much improved. The doctors and nurses were all astounded.

Leah stayed in the ICU but made daily progress. I was quickly recovering and my doctor said I could go home. However, Dr. Brown, Leah's doctor, intervened. Leah had severe stomach problems and needed to be nursed often. He went to the hospital administrator and my doctor and explained that if I went home, it would be too exhausting and would deplete me. Leah needed me to recover. He was concerned that the stress of running back and forth to the hospital to care for Leah would compromise my health and my milk supply. A week later we were both able to go home. Leah had to be nursed every two hours, and we weren't allowed to leave home during those first several weeks of her life, but all was good. I learned an important truth that night in the hospital when I was alone with the Lord and very new in this "God walk." I learned that to surrender to the Lord is the best thing I can do in any crisis. His heart is to bless me. Since that day, there have been many times that God has reminded me that my children are His, and my position is to hold them with an open hand. Through our experience with Leah, God was teaching us to trust Him. He was growing us and helping us to learn to surrender ourselves and our plans to Him. This was a brand new experience for us. We were beginning to understand that when hard things came, it didn't mean God was unhappy with us. He was growing us, refining us, and trusting us with the stewardship of bringing honor to Him in difficult circumstances.

After Leah arrived, my life was very different. I was home all day with my little girls. My career ambitions were totally gone. They belonged to another person who was dead and gone. A new person was alive in me. Every day I looked out at the large number of children in our neighborhood who came home from school without a parent to greet them. Most of the tenants in our complex were career people and both parents worked. My heart was moved for the children, and I realized that on Sundays nearly no one else in the complex went to church. I began to pray for the families around me. Many of them were living the very life that God had specifically called us to leave. There was a stirring in my heart to make a difference.

God gave me an idea. I baked cookies every Monday with the windows open, sending forth yummy smells from my apartment. As children wandered by or played with my children, I'd share a cookie with the promise of more tomorrow if they would meet me at the pool house for stories, games, and crafts. Knowing this was too big for me, I called my friend Becky, and Bible Club began. The children came for the cookies, listened intently to the Bible stories, enjoyed the fun crafts, and many left with Jesus. As a new believer in my first ministry, I had no idea that this was amazing. I just knew that God had called me to bake cookies and to pray for my neighbors. My days were full as I cared for my family and made preparations for Bible Club each week. It was a good season. Life was not without problems as we continued to recover financially, but God was allowing us to make a difference. New children came every week. Parents were happy for their children to have a fun activity. Each week, the children took home their crafts to show to their families, and the Word of God was hidden securely in their hearts. Being used by God was also making a difference in us. He was allowing us the privilege of being His tool in the lives of others. Years later, a pastor's wife came to me and shared that her son was dating a young lady. When she asked this young lady about her relationship with Jesus, the girl shared that she had received Christ in Bible Club years earlier. How sweet of the Lord to allow me to see His investment in this young lady's life. I was beginning to understand that the call to be a "fruitful vine within my house" was not simply for the benefit of my family. Looking back, I see this as a connecting dot to WLFJ. Something as small as a cookie or a bag of groceries can be used by Holy Spirit God to show the love of Christ and to build His Kingdom!

Chapter 3
Learning to Walk His Path of Obedience

Oh, the depth of the riches of the wisdom and knowledge of God!
How unsearchable his judgments, and his paths beyond tracing out!
Romans 11:33, NIV

Jesus shows up in the most unusual places. A stable in Bethlehem, a dusty old warehouse, a little outdated house in the middle of an affluent neighborhood. The Lord reminded me one Christmas that the stable was for our benefit. He left the glories of heaven to come to this earth. The cleanest, most pristine place on the planet would be like a stable compared to heaven. The location He chose to enter our world helps us understand just a tiny bit of what He experienced and gave up for us!

Two years later the apartment complex was sold and along with it went Sam's job again. Where our last move had been an upgrade, the next one we had to make was quite different. This new place was affordable, but not a family-friendly environment. After moving in, we realized there was illegal activity taking place in the apartment beside ours. We were on guard, especially on the weekends when unhealthy activities filled the parking lot. We quickly decided this would be a short-term solution. As we sought the Lord's direction and Sam looked for a new job, we realized that though having a combined employment and living situation had been great for our transition period, it was not the best for us in the long term. Leaving this era of our lives was a place of expectancy and sadness. God had shown Himself to be faithful to us those past few years. We had enjoyed rich ministry among our neighbors, especially with the Bible Club. The adventure with Him had been great, even though it was not always easy. This move didn't happen as quickly or as easily as the last one. It was obvious that God had us on a different training ground now. Sam found a job, and we looked for an affordable place to live. Our options were very limited. We packed up and moved into a tiny, two-bedroom apartment within walking distance of our former apartment complex. We were starting over again. The decision for me not to work outside the home was always hard. With our three girls to support and a lot of pre-Christ mistakes to work out, obedience was our constant hope and focus. We came to realize that our step of faith meant looking for, and expecting God to show up in our daily lives. We had one car which Sam drove to work. Grocery shopping was limited to what I could carry in the stroller as the girls and I walked to do most of our errands. Life had many challenges, but God was faithful.

Just before the buy-out on the apartment complex happened, a new family had moved into our building. Marcia and I became friends. Her husband was a police officer and they had two small children close to Leah's age. Her life was extremely difficult, and their marriage was on rocky ground. Her husband had disengaged from their family and obviously had deep personal problems. She watched God at work in our lives during the sale of the apartment complex, Sam looking for a new job, and our eventual move. God was at work in her life, too. She asked a lot of questions. She saw God show up and make provision for our family. She longed for a different life for her own family.

One morning after we moved to the smaller place, the Lord burdened me to go visit her and talk to her about her need for

Jesus in her life. I was quite intimidated by her husband and knew he would likely be home. The Holy Spirit continued to press me. Tara was at school. I put Leah in the stroller and started walking the short distance to Marcia's apartment. I cried out to the Lord, asking that Marcia be in the parking lot when I arrived. I didn't want to have to knock on her door. I didn't want to deal with her husband and his possible anger. As I got closer, I could see her parking area. She was not outside. I prayed, setting my heart to be obedient, and gingerly started to walk down the steps that led to her apartment. Just as I took the first step, I heard a car pull into the parking lot and a door open. I turned to see Marcia stepping out of her car. I hadn't even noticed that her car was not there.

We talked in the parking lot for a few minutes as I shared with her my concern that she was trying to make it without Jesus in her life. We got back into her car and drove to my house where I called my pastor. A few minutes later we were on our way to his house for them to talk. A couple of hours later we headed back home. She was full of questions. I assumed that she had received Christ, though she never said so. Over the next weeks she called me multiple times a day with numerous questions. I was forced into the Word to stay ahead of her questions. I had never been in that position. It was a new place for me to cry out to the Lord for His wisdom and guidance. One day, as we were talking, she mentioned to me that until she'd visited with the pastor, she hadn't realized that you have to ask Jesus to be your Savior. I asked her if she had done that. She changed the subject and didn't answer my question. The next day she called to tell me that she had gone home that day and received Christ. This started a discipling time for me as I helped her in this new walk with the Lord. She not only became a good friend, but also God's great tool for growth and discipleship in my life. God works in wondrous ways! Marcia continued to walk with the Lord and live the life of Christ before her husband. In spite of her godly testimony, he eventually deserted their family. As Marcia grew in her relationship, God began to unfold His plan for her family. Several years later, He brought a godly widower with three children into her life and they blended into a beautiful family. God later called them into full-time ministry. God definitely called me to witness to and disciple Marcia, but He also called her into my life for my growth. I'm always amazed at how God takes our simple obedience and turns it around for blessing us. His love for us is greater than we can comprehend.

As our family walked this place of yet another transition, a friend from church who lived in a duplex told us that the other side would soon be available. Every day I looked out my door to see drug deals going down and was afraid to allow my little girls outside alone. It seemed that the busiest traffic next door was during the lunch hour, so I would close our curtains and doors, and the girls and I would rest or read until the noon hour passed each day. At night when Sam was working, I would balance a Pepsi bottle upside down in front of the doors, so I'd be alerted if someone broke into the house during the night. The thought of a Christian neighbor, a larger place, and a nice yard for the girls to play in seemed like a perfect dream come true. We submitted an application for the duplex. We were shocked, disappointed, and confused when we were turned down. The landlord seemed to like us and was very friendly when we had visited our friends, yet for some reason the application was turned down. This made absolutely no sense to me. Why would God want us to stay in this place when there was a better and even more affordable place for us to live?

Sam was working two jobs. As I prayed and cried late one night, trying to understand why this opportunity was denied us, the Lord spoke: *I declare to you that the Lord will build a house for you...* (1 Chronicles 17:10). It seemed that those words jumped off the page at me as though they were somehow highlighted. I read and re-read the chapter and it happened again and again. I asked the Lord if this meant that He had something better for us. He confirmed in my spirit that He had a house for us. I couldn't wait to share this with Sam when he got home. We had no idea how to make this happen, but believed He was faithful to do what He had said. As I look back at the road God had called us to walk, I am amazed at His great ability to communicate with us. We were growing in the Lord and seeking Him, but we had no real discipleship. He had obviously taken on the responsibility of growing us in our walk with Him.

One Wednesday night at church, a friend excitedly shared with me that her family had purchased a new house. I was so delighted for her. We had visited her once in her current home. It was an older farmhouse-type dwelling on a couple of acres of land, set back from a busy thoroughfare. Her eyes lit up with excitement as she seemed to have an idea. She asked me if we would be interested in renting it from the owner. He was a retired sheriff's deputy that lived out of state and just wanted someone to take care of the house where he and his wife had raised their family. The house held a lot of sentimental value to him, and he loved the idea of a family with young children living there. He had asked her if she knew someone who might be a potential renter. She suddenly found herself thinking of our family as a possibility. The rent was an unheard-of $165 per month, with no deposit, no application fee, and no lease. It had three bedrooms, one bath, and was very old. In my heart, I knew this was *the* house! God was teaching us that sometimes He says "no" because He has a better plan.

My friend made contact with the owner and within a few days we had confirmation that he was delighted with the idea. We began to plan for yet another move. God was teaching us to trust Him, to wait on His provision, and to clearly hear Him speak. Our girls, who currently shared a bedroom, would have their own rooms and a huge yard with lots of anticipated adventures. At church the next week I shared with an older, more mature Christian about my crying out to God and Him telling me He had a house for us. She kept asking me questions and seemed to doubt that God had spoken to me in such a strange way. I was so excited over God's word to us and His plan unfolding that her concern for my immaturity didn't even faze me. My God was fighting for me and I was resting in that truth! I was quite sure I didn't know all I should know, but He was growing me. I was very thankful!

As time went by, I learned that God develops with each of us

His own way of speaking and making Himself known to us individually. There is no magic formula, and no wrong way if God is in it. When God speaks, we sometimes begin to imagine how things will look. His plan is often very different from our imagination, but it's always right and good. All we could imagine was a house, lots of play space for the children, no drug deals, and the amazing knowledge that this was God's provision for us. We were excited as we loaded up our old car and a borrowed truck, and drove away from the drug infested neighborhood and tiny two-bedroom apartment. We pulled into a graveled circular drive and saw an overgrown but beautiful two-acre yard with lavish, purple, fragrant wisteria hanging in the woods, huge oak trees perfect for climbing (one would soon be named the "talking tree"), sweet-smelling honeysuckle garnishing the unshaped shrubs, and a wonderful, L-shaped front porch complete with a swing.

We stepped onto old, dingy carpet to find walls with high ceilings that needed painting, a bathroom ceiling covered with black mold, a dirty basement, and a huge attic filled with the owners "stuff." The kitchen appliances were relics, but the cabinets were amazing (the last tenant had been a carpenter). A window air-conditioning unit in the dining room was the only air-conditioning for the house, but there were lots of doors, windows, and shade trees. A new adventure was ahead of us and another connecting dot to WLFJ. Many years later, we would step into a huge 116,000 square foot shopping center on the south side of Raleigh that was basically deserted with no air-conditioning, no heat, no electricity, and again have the Lord confirm in our spirits that this was the place He had been promising to house His ministry. We would understand that the important common denominator about the dusty old warehouse, the outdated farmhouse, and the smelly stable was that Jesus, for some unknown reason, showed up in all of these unlikely places to make Himself known, to be worshiped, to be enjoyed, and to direct a work He called into being. There was nothing special about the people or the places. Jesus! His Presence made these places special. What was lacking in décor was more than compensated for with Jesus!

God was helping our family to learn dependence on Him. There was so much we didn't know or understand, but we were on His training ground. Sam washed the bathroom ceiling down with bleach. It looked clean and new. We cleaned the carpet the best we could and did our best to clean up the basement. The yard got a fresh mowing and we added a kitty to our family. We were settling in to our new life. One day while at work, Sam noticed a paint crew throwing gallons of paint into the dumpster. He had no idea what color it was, but when he inquired he was told it was too old to use. With several gallons of that paint in hand, he started the task of painting our "new to us" house. The paint made the house look and smell fresh, and the color was perfect. The kitchen appliances were included with the house; however, the owner told us if they quit working, he would not replace them. We were welcome to use them as long as they would last. Leah had a small adjustment to being in her own room and all the creaks and noises of an old house, but very soon we all settled into this "new" place of God's provision. *Boundary lines had fallen for us in pleasant places* (Psalm 16:6, NIV).

A few months after we moved into the farmhouse, we were expecting my cousin, Sandra, and her family to come for a visit. We hadn't seen them since we'd moved into the house and were excited for their visit. The last time they'd visited with us had been a memorable experience. Sandra's husband, John, was confined to a wheelchair. As a young police officer in Baltimore, he was shot during a shootout with a man on drugs. Their lives had forever changed as he would spend the rest of his life paralyzed. Sandra had visited me right after his injury, and at that time, she had received Christ as her Savior. Then sometime later, they invited us to spend Easter with them in Florida. We had traveled together for a great vacation. Sam and I prayed that John would receive Christ during that visit. When we returned from the trip, though John had asked lots of questions and we had great discussions, he had still not made a decision for Jesus. I watched them drive away that day and cried because I so wanted him to know Christ and to see God redeem John's life. Every day was difficult for John. I knew God could give him a life that would be good and valuable. I later learned that as he was driving home that day, with his family asleep in the van, he cried out to the Lord for salvation. During their visit this time, they would go with us to church, and we would be able to continue our great friendship on a new level—as brothers and sisters in Christ. Now that Sam and I were walking with the Lord, it was so important to us that the people in our lives knew Him, too. Many years later, Sam and I would stand beside John's bed, knowing he would soon slip into the presence of the Lord, and we would give thanks to the Lord for allowing us to be a small part in sowing that seed into John's life.

I had been buying groceries, cooking, and preparing for John and Sandra's visit when, without warning, the refrigerator just stopped. Sam is the ultimate fix-it man, but this refrigerator was beyond even his ability to repair. There was a man in our church who worked for an appliance store. Sam called him and asked if they sold used refrigerators. We knew we couldn't afford a new one, but hoped that a used one might be a possibility. The man asked Sam who needed a refrigerator and Sam explained our situation. This man's family had *that day* purchased a new refrigerator, and their old one worked fine. They were simply upgrading to something newer and were looking for a place to pass on their old one. He was so very blessed to pass it on to us, and we were so excited by this wonderful provision of God. It was old to them, but new to us—certainly much newer than what we had been using. That refrigerator was still working when we moved away from that house many years later. God has provisions that we know nothing about and His ways are perfect. In days to come, there would be many times at WLFJ when we would pray for God's provision for someone who needed an appliance or other item. We would not have one available, but would encourage them that God had heard our prayer. Many times while they were shopping for other items, we would find that exactly what we had prayed for had just been delivered to our loading dock and the prayer had been answered. It's so much fun to watch God at work!

Our family continued to go through many seasons, like our guests at WLFJ, where we would have a need and Jesus would send that provision at the perfect time. I was tucking Tara into bed one night when she asked me a question.

"Mom, is it wrong to ask Jesus for a new coat if you already have one?"

I answered her by saying, "Jesus loves for us to ask Him for the things we need and want. It's always fine to ask."

She had a winter coat, but it was one that she had "inherited" and was not very stylish. There was a certain type coat that she really wanted. We prayed together, sharing this with the Lord. The next day I went to the refrigerator to take out a piece of meat to cook for dinner. It was a really nice pork loin that I had splurged to buy at the grocery store. We were going to get several meals off this large piece of meat. When I opened it, it was spoiled. I took it back to the grocery store and got my money back. Later that day, I shared Tara's request with Sam. He told me to take the money from the meat and go to Belk, find a coat for Tara, and use the money to put it on layaway. (I still can't remember what we ate for dinner.) I emptied our "penny" jar to add to my little stash. When I got to Belk they were having a huge clearance sale. On one of their clearance racks was *the coat*. It was the only one on the rack and it was Tara's size. It was on sale for exactly what I had in my purse. A piece of spoiled meat and a penny jar became the answer to Tara's prayer. Jesus continued to show up in our lives again and again.

It was Christmastime in 1983. Christmas brought with it extra need in a family already struggling with finances. There was no provision for Christmas. Early one morning, as I was spending time with the Lord, He told me that before the day was over, we'd see His provision for the children's Christmas. The Lord also gave me Psalm 37:3-4: *Trust in the Lord and do good; dwell in the land and enjoy safe pasture. Delight yourself in the Lord and he will give you the desires of your heart.* He told me to look for how I could bless others. My willingness to do good to others would reveal that I trusted Him to take care of what I was not able to do for myself. I couldn't see anything to do to help others and nothing was coming to my mind, but I asked Him to open my eyes to see what He had in mind. Tara was at school. Leah and I were getting our day started. The Lord reminded me how much Ms. Marge, one of our neighbors, loved to bake. We had been given a large bag of pecans and Sam had shelled them out for me. (He still is the best pecan cracker in the world.) I called Ms. Marge and Leah and I went for a visit with a container of these beautiful pecans to share. It was a lovely visit, and it was obvious that Ms. Marge needed the visit as much as she'd enjoyed the nuts. Later, back at home, I pulled a jar of homemade applesauce down from its perch on top of the cabinets to add to lunch for Leah and me. The Lord brought to mind Ms. Leslie, my landlord's sister, who lived a couple miles away. She was an older widow and had just had surgery and was limited to only soft foods. This applesauce would be perfect for her. Leah and I tied ribbon around a big jar and headed to Ms. Leslie's house. She, too, was blessed by the yummy gift (she had often picked apples from our yard when her brother lived there,) and the visit of a little girl.

It was getting to be late afternoon when Becky called and asked if I could help with her Bible Club. Tara was home to help with Leah, and I had dinner ready to put on the table whenever Sam arrived home. I called Sam at work to see if he was good with me driving our car to the other side of town to help with the club, as this little bit of gas had to last us for several more days. His employer had supplied him with a truck to drive back and forth to work because he was always on call, but it could not be driven for personal use. He was fine with it. Tara would put dinner on the table with his help, and I'd be home soon after the club was over.

As I drove to meet my friend, my mind wandered back to the promise God had made earlier in the day. I wondered if Sam would come home with some unexpected money or how else I was going to see God's provision. I had to fight the temptation to doubt His word to me that morning. It's hard work to take thoughts captive and bring them into the submission of what God has said. He filled me with hope and expectancy. God was not a teaser! He was at work! I could trust Him to do what He had said. It was not up to me to figure out how He would do it.

I had fun helping with the club. Afterwards, we cleaned up and got everything in order. Becky asked if I could run by her house for a minute before I headed home. Things at home were well-covered, so I had time. We stepped into her living room and there was the cutest little kitchen set I'd ever seen. It was used but looked almost new. (Looking down the path to WLFJ, we would call this "gently" used.) Someone had called her earlier that day and asked if she'd like to have it for her daughter who was two years younger than Leah. When she went to get it, she felt that her daughter wouldn't really appreciate it yet. She told her friend about our family and asked if she could share it with us, knowing that down the road, she'd get it back. Her friend not only gave her the little kitchen but put some cash in her hands and told her to bless us with that as well.

I sang all the way home. I had Leah's Christmas present in the back of the car and enough cash in my hand to buy Tara and Lesly a Christmas gift with some leftover. That little kitchen was going to be such a treat for Leah. I couldn't wait to tell Sam and see his expression as he looked at God's rich provision for us. When I arrived home, I found a very discouraged Sam. He'd suffered an eye injury that day at work, had been to the doctor, and was given a prescription that needed to be filled. He knew we had no money to get the medication. I now had enough money to get the medication he needed, take care of the Christmas needs for our children, and put a little gas back in the car. God had done an amazing multiplication act. Sam was surprised and delighted with this timely and unexpected provision. The feelings of hopelessness and discouragement were gone. He was as excited with the little kitchen for Leah as I was, and also with the ability to meet the needs in our household. I have always been so blessed by this man that God has given me to walk with on planet earth. Sam came into our marriage expecting a partner that would work outside the home. He was now carrying the responsibilities of caring for our three little girls and the recovery from our past as he freed me up to be the "fruitful vine within the house" to bless our family and others.

In late January we were given the gift of a big turkey. I always canned vegetables in the summer. My friend Linda taught me how to can and showed me the places to glean vegetables from fields or the places where picking was inexpensive. We gathered all the fruit from our yard—apples, grapes, plums, etc. With the gift of the turkey, I wanted to prepare a meal and invite my parents to dinner. They were not believers (later I would find out that my mom did know the Lord, and my dad received Christ before he died). We did not share our hard places with them. We knew that they thought I should be working and our lifestyle was a stretch for them to even begin to understand. My dad was a wonderful businessman who had built his little paint business into a very successful one, and my mom had always worked. For them, coming out of the depression and having great work ethics, our lifestyle made no sense at all. When we had needs, we went to the Lord with them. We didn't discuss these needs with others and especially not my parents. We never wanted to be a burden to them or cause them to be worried about us. They loved us and wanted the best for us. Because of their own pasts, they just couldn't process that the best for us might not mean financial prosperity. When they looked at their own broken pasts, growing up in difficult and needy families, it seemed to them that money would've solved all their problems. I could definitely understand how they felt that way. They wanted much more for their children than the hardships they had endured. The brokenness in their heritage included a lack of funds, but the lack was much deeper than money.

The oil drum outside the kitchen window fed our antique heating system. I asked Sam if he'd dip the stick into the drum to see how much oil we had. I knew it was getting very low and the last thing I wanted was for it to run out while my parents were visiting for the evening. He checked the drum and felt there would likely be enough for at least a couple more days. We were praying for more, but so far we hadn't seen the provision.

With everything now covered, I called my parents and invited them to come to dinner. We were going to have a feast—

yummy turkey along with green beans, applesauce, squash, scalloped tomatoes from our summer canning, and homemade sweet potato pie. It was all coming together when I heard an all too familiar noise. The pump on the heating system stopped. I ran to check the oil. The drum was empty. There was no way to buy more, and my parents would be coming in a couple of hours. This house with no insulation would get cold quickly. All we could do was cry out to the Lord. Dinner was ready, my parents arrived, and we had a lovely visit with them. The house never got cold. They never knew there was a problem. I cleaned up the kitchen and headed to bed realizing that the house was not uncomfortable. The Lord covered the house all night. We never were cold and the next day He provided a way for us to get more oil. His faithfulness is new every single day! In our walk with the Lord, we see individual circumstances, but God sees something different. He is busily connecting the dots of life and preparing us for the next step with Him. Each day of our lives helps to equip us for another day of walking with the Lord. One faith step builds on the next. Each step of obedience becomes a storehouse that we can go to for future decisions or for ways to encourage others. As we walked what seemed to us like very ordinary days with the King of Glory, He was equipping and preparing us to encourage the honored guests who would show up one day at WLFJ looking for help. Nothing is wasted with our God!

One spring evening in 1984, Sam came home from work in an unusually good mood. He always had a joke or a funny story to share with me, but this day he was even more upbeat than usual. When I asked why he was in such a good mood, he said, "I ran out of gas today." I didn't understand. Sam ran out of gas and somehow this was the reason for his good mood? This was too crazy. He said the fuel was very low in the car, but he had to drive it across town to get a part he needed, and the car ran out of gas. He went on to share that he got out and starting walking down the road with no money to buy more gas. (This was obviously before cell phone days.) He was walking along, mumbling to himself and the Lord as he was kicking the ground at the same time. Suddenly one of those kicks uprooted a stone, and with it, a ten-dollar bill. He stood in astonishment as he looked at this unexpected provision from God. He picked up the cash and thanked the Lord. He walked to the service station and borrowed a gasoline can with a little gas in it, and then walked back to the car. He drove back to the store, returned the can, and put gas in the car. God showed up in his day. Little things became big things and even greater reasons to celebrate the Lord's goodness to us. He was providing for our physical needs, building connecting dots for a future time, but also at work to heal and restore us.

Chapter 4
Entertaining Angels

Don't forget to show hospitality to strangers, for some who have done
this have entertained angels without realizing it!
Hebrews 13:2, NLT

One day a simple phone call became an opportunity for Jesus to redeem and heal a part of our past. Larry, a pastor friend, called to tell me he was part of a small group of believers who were praying about opening a crisis pregnancy center in Raleigh. He was led to call me to see if I would like to join them. What he didn't know was that I had experienced a crisis pregnancy. Today we live in very different times, but being pregnant and unmarried was not an acceptable thing in the early 70s. I didn't know where to turn. There didn't seem to be any safe or good place to go to for help when I found myself in this very difficult situation. Sam's aunt had invited us to attend church with her. We had gone a few times. I went to see her with this unacceptable crisis. Abortion was not legal in North Carolina at the time, so it was not even an option that I had considered. His aunt slipped a piece of paper into my hand with a phone number on it. She said if I would call this number, they would help me get rid of my problem. I was surprised by her response to my need. I'm not sure what I expected, but definitely didn't expect the only Christian I knew at the time to give me this advice. There was no conviction in my heart that abortion was either right or wrong. I was not a believer, and I certainly never expected myself to be in this type of situation. On my lunch hour at work the next day, I called the number. When the receptionist answered, I had the thought that if this was illegal, it must be wrong. I hung up the phone and cried. (That same thought wouldn't work today!) I know now that even then, in my lost condition, God was watching over me and this precious life within me.

Sam and I quickly slipped away in the middle of the night to be married by the justice of the peace. I went to the doctor for my first appointment and my blood pressure was very high. Every time I went, it was elevated. The doctor kept warning me that whatever was going on that was making me so anxious needed to stop because I was not going to live through delivery with this severe blood pressure problem. Her "threats" were not helping my situation at all. I knew the disgrace that my parents would feel and knew my dad's temper would likely explode in anger and disapproval when he found out about my pregnancy. My parents would add to my already great shame. I would be labeled by my friends when they found out. I couldn't deal with the pressure. Soon thereafter, we moved to another state to have our baby. My new doctor was very understanding and assured me that everything would be fine. Far away from home with few people in our lives, our baby was born safe and healthy, and to my amazement, I lived! I cannot imagine what life would have been like for me without my precious Tara. God is incredible in His care for us. We moved back to Raleigh and began a new life with our baby. Sam's aunt never asked me about it. I suspect that she was embarrassed that she even suggested such a thing and was thankful that I did not heed her advice. So, I joined Larry's group. As a team, we sought God's provision for a crisis pregnancy ministry, and God made a way.

In a few months, I stepped into a new place of ministry. What

I also found was a place of healing and restoration for me. As I took the training to be a counselor for the crisis pregnancy center, it became a place of understanding, forgiveness, and acceptance for me. Yes, God had called me into a new place of service, but He had also called this ministry to be His tool for a place in me that needed His touch. All my sin was forgiven when I received Christ; however, I needed to forgive myself and deal with this time in my life. I needed to let go of the shame, and welcome God into this hurtful place for His redemption and healing. I loved working with the young ladies that came to the crisis center. I could relate. I didn't receive Christ until I was 28, so I understood what it was like to waste years and feel hopeless about the future. It was very exciting to share Jesus and watch Him at work in their lives. This was also my first exposure to the greater Body of Christ outside my local church.

One of my good friends, Lee, became the director of the center. Together we had the privilege of helping lay a foundation for this ministry. God was at work in us as He also chose to use us. It was fun, challenging, refining, and rewarding. I loved serving with Lee. She was very upbeat and positive. My family heritage was riddled with negativity. Until I was exposed to Lee on a near daily basis, I didn't realize what a stronghold negativity was in my life. God used this precious sister in Christ, by her example, to reveal to me an area of my life that needed to come under the Lordship of Jesus. It continues to be a place that God is at work in me.

I had my first real exposure to denominational differences at the center and found it to be more exciting than challenging. These diverse believers stimulated my thinking and caused me to dig deeper into God's Word for answers. I loved serving with people from many different churches and backgrounds. Of course I had no idea at the time what a big connecting dot this would be to WLFJ.

Our family became more and more involved at the crisis center. After-hours phone calls were often forwarded to our home. We had many opportunities to pray for young ladies in crisis. From the old storehouse of our pain, God was giving our family opportunities for ministry. He is so good! My girls learned early in life to value life and understood God's position about abortion. This offered great opportunities for us to have open and honest discussions in our home. It was a few days before Christmas of 1985. I answered the phone at the center to hear a young girl crying on the other end. I prayed aloud for her, asked her to take a couple of deep breaths and just start talking to me. Whatever was wrong, there was a solution. She quieted a bit and told me her name was Denise and that she was in labor and very afraid. Her parents were both at work and didn't know she was pregnant. She said she wore baggy sweatshirts and was able to keep them from knowing about her pregnancy. Even that morning her mom had expressed concern, questioning why her tummy was getting so big and why she was gaining weight. She avoided her mom's eyes and questions.

By her breathing and the fast coming contractions I could tell that her baby was soon to arrive. She gave me her address which I handed to another volunteer at the center with a note to please call EMS. She gave me her parents' names and their work phone numbers. We prayed together and chatted until the EMS workers arrived. They quickly took her to the hospital. She was so worried about what her parents would do, and was upset because she had not yet shopped for her mother's Christmas present. I assured her that I would come see her at the hospital and take care of that shopping for her. It's strange the things that consume us in a crisis! After we hung up, I prayed for her parents and made one of the hardest phone calls I've ever made. I first tried to call her mother, but she was not available. I called her dad. He seemed distracted at first, trying to figure out who I was and why I was calling. I could hear the pain in his voice as he realized what was happening. His voice began to break as he awkwardly thanked me for the phone call. By this time, Tara was a young teen about the same age of this girl. I was moved with compassion for these parents, though I knew I couldn't enter into their place of pain. As I visited her the next day at the hospital, she hugged me for a long time as her dad stood by with huge tears filling his eyes. He assured her that he would take care of her shopping, but her baby was a beautiful Christmas gift for their family. My heart went out to him as I knew he was still in shock and was struggling to support his wayward daughter. This was a well-educated, affluent family, and like everyone in such a crisis, they never expected to be in this situation. I shared the good news of Jesus with them and slipped away to leave the results with the Holy Spirit.

So often at WLFJ, we are blessed to step into the lives of those in great crisis and meet the need of the moment, share Jesus, and trust Holy Spirit God to continue to work. God continues to connect the dots.

* * *

Our family was learning to walk with God, and we were growing together. Sam and I had very little family heritage in this area to draw on. We appreciated those people and books that God gave us to stimulate our thinking, our growth, and our sensitivity to Holy Spirit God. We had family night once a week with the children. We would go skating, or visit a shut in, or go on a picnic, or play games at home. The purpose in this time was to build and strengthen our family. On one of those evenings, God gave us our "family verse." *Don't forget to entertain strangers, for in so doing some have entertained angels without knowing it* (Hebrews 13:2). There would be many times over the years that we would wonder if we had just "entertained angels."

Many years down the road there was a time in particular that stands out to me. Leah was just beginning her school experience as a freshman in high school (having been homeschooled until then). I dropped her off that first day with a heavy heart and constant anxiety for her. A high school filled with thousands of students was very different from studying at the family's kitchen table. As I pulled away from the school, I saw an unusual looking woman walking down the sidewalk with a gasoline can in her hand. She was dressed in worn clothes but was not unkempt. I was struck by her pleasant countenance in what appeared to be a difficult circumstance. She didn't appear to be homeless, yet seemed somehow fragile and sturdy at the same time. As I passed her and drove on down the road, Holy Spirit God continued to keep her in my mind's eye. I turned my car around and stopped to ask her if I could help. She spoke softly, telling me that her car was out of gas. She climbed in my car and we went to the service station. She had no money. I had very little. I took most of what I had and filled the can with gas. We went to her car which was parked behind a deserted building. She used her hand as a funnel as I poured the gas into her tank. Looking at her car, I realized that she was homeless—living out of her car. There was a McDonald's next door. I used the last of my money to get her a biscuit and a cup of coffee. She received it with sweet eyes that penetrated my soul. I drove away and the Lord said, "Angel unaware." The Lord sent her to me to get my attention away from myself and Leah. He used her to fill my heart with gratitude. This experience and many others would confirm to our family this precious verse God had given us.

Along our path with Jesus, Sam had back surgery in 1986. Actually, he would eventually have seven, but he had three back surgeries in eighteen months and was out of work for a long time. I asked Sam if I should find a job during this time. His response was that we needed to wait. God had directed me to stay home, and we didn't need to let circumstances cause us to make a decision opposite from God's instruction to us. My special friend Julia came to me one day knowing that life must be difficult with Sam out of work. Her brother had died recently and she had received a small inheritance from his estate. She and I had served together at the crisis center and went to the same church. We had become great friends. I loved her frank conversations and her love for Jesus. She wanted to use the money from her brother's estate to bless others. Sam was going to be out of work for six months with this last surgery. She wrote me six rent checks made out to my landlord dated for the next six months. She also wrote six checks and gave them to Tara. Each month Tara was to cash a check and use it for lunch money and her allowance until her daddy was back on his feet. It was obvious that God was looking for ways to bless us. Yes, these were difficult days, but He had us by the hand. During this same period of time, we would wake up every other Saturday morning to find a box on the front porch with fresh vegetables and other treats. We never knew where these boxes came from, but it ended when Sam went back to work. Years later we found out who delivered the boxes but never knew the provider. God honored Sam's obedience and humility. This was not an easy place for a big, strong man to have to accept, but he did!

* * *

As the crisis center continued to serve the community, Laura came with her own crisis. She was pregnant, unmarried, and her mom and stepfather would not allow her to stay with them unless she killed her baby. One of the services we hoped to provide was shepherding homes for young women that needed a place to live so they could carry their babies to term. Laura was the first one to come with such a need. I never considered our home an option. We had three bedrooms but only one bath. Our girls were eight and sixteen at the time so sharing a room was difficult. The house was very cold in the winter with an old heating system and very high ceilings. After our first winter in the house when the temperature didn't reach above fifty degrees some days, we had to purchase a couple of kerosene heaters that we moved around the house to supplement our inadequate furnace. Summers were not as difficult but insufficient air-conditioning didn't work well for pregnant ladies. God had other thoughts. He began to move our hearts to offer Laura a place to live. Our argument with God was that she was from an upper middle-class family and was accustomed to a much nicer living space than what we had to offer. He was not buying our argument. We had a family meeting. Tara was the one in the most difficult place. Sharing her room with a messy little sister was not going to be easy. God was really stretching us! We prayed together and understood that we were being asked to share what we cherished most—our family.

As a part of the shepherding process, the center made contact with our pastor to hear his thoughts about us housing a young woman in our home. Our pastor said kind things about us as a family, but was concerned about the negative effects that housing these young ladies would have on our small and very impressionable daughters. We were about to learn that obedience is the safest place to live. God was showing us to simply obey Him and leave the outcome to Him. The amazing thing is that the more we obey, the more we open ourselves up for real intimacy with Jesus. *Whoever has my commands and obeys them, he is the one who loves me. He who loves me will be loved by my Father, and I too will love him and show myself to him* (John 14:21). We knew that our pastor and church family loved us and were simply concerned for us, but we had to obey regardless of what others might think.

I invited Laura to visit our home. Her family actually lived in one of the beautiful housing developments near us. She was not a believer. We shared Jesus with her. She really wanted to give birth to her baby, though she was unsure whether she should place it for adoption or raise the baby herself. She accepted our offer. Leah moved into Tara's room and gave Laura hers. All of Leah's toys were placed on shelves in the large dining room which became her play space. She slept with Tara. One day, as we were running errands together, Laura began to share with me her concern for her uncle who was very ill. She was worried about his salvation. The conversation was so strange to me because she had not received Christ for herself. I could see that God was at work in her life. Laura was visiting her family one night a few weeks before Emerald, her daughter, was born. She called me from their home and asked me not to go to bed before she returned. She needed to talk to me. That night, huddled by the fireplace sipping hot tea, Laura and I talked and prayed together. She asked Jesus to take her sins away and give her a new life. We were all very excited. Laura and her daughter would have a very different life. We were thankful as a family that we had offered our home to the Lord.

Soon little Emerald also joined our household and life stepped up a new and fast notch. Before Emerald's birth, Laura enjoyed our girls and loved having them around. Once her baby arrived, Laura was critical and aggravated with them—especially with Leah. God was just preparing her to move into her own space and live apart from us. It was all good, but certainly not always pleasant. One day Leah came to me and asked how much longer it would be before Laura and her baby moved out. We had agreed for her to stay with us until her baby was three months old so she could get back to work and on her feet. She would have been with us a total of nine months. I held Leah on my lap and we talked about the time left. She said to me, "Mommy, I didn't realize nine months could be so long." I think we all agreed with her! Again God was showing us that *"your wife will be like a fruitful vine within your house..."* was not just a provision for our family but for others as well. We were learning commitment not an easy concept! God was doing a work in our family that was an important connecting dot to a future time in our own family, but also a future time at WLFJ.

What we didn't realize at the time was that Laura and little Emerald would be the first of many young ladies and children that would come to live with us over the next twenty years. Our girls would spend much of their childhood sharing their home with others. It did cost us something, but the rewards of obedience are great. Deposits into a future time were made. We were simply living life as God directed. We had no idea that we were also learning important truths for a later place of ministry. God was teaching us then and for many years later that every place of need becomes an opportunity for Jesus to be made known and His Kingdom to be built.

Chapter 5
Truth—God's Path to Healing and Freedom

Direct your children onto the right path, and when they are older,
they will not leave it.
Proverbs 22:6, NLT

When Leah was around seven, our family headed to the beach for a week. I was struggling in my walk with the Lord. Comparing myself with others, feeling like a failure, vague feelings of not measuring up, and general uneasiness were all things I dealt with regularly. In time these and more struggles would make sense to me, but at that time it was unsettling. I wanted to know how to show my love to Jesus in a deeper way. I ran across a book that caught my attention and decided to take it with me to the beach. It was *Loving God* by Chuck Colson. My great take away from that book was that obedience shows that we love God. As I grew in my relationship with the Lord, I increasingly understood that after salvation, obedience is the next step in building a relationship with God. The more I tuned my heart to hear God speak, and honored Him in quick obedience, the more that relationship of love grew. Obedience was a stepping stone to help me better understand the Father's heart, and it opened doors of opportunity for Him to invite me to be a part of His work. It became increasingly amazing to have God share with me things He planned to do, or His view about something. The truth is, if I have a problem with obedience in any area of my life, it reflects that I need to know my great God better. Lack of obedience can often be a trust issue. But the more I know Him, the more automatic obedience becomes because I'm able to walk in a relationship based on trust. I set my heart to walk in an obedient love relationship with the Lord.

Another interesting thing happened as a result of reading Colson's book. God spoke to me and gave me a burden to get involved in the prison. I'd never had any thoughts of being involved in prison ministry and certainly had no idea of how to even begin. I told the Lord that I would be obedient. I needed Him to bring something or someone to me. I thought I'd probably look for a way to be a pen pal to someone in prison. God had other plans.

We returned home from the beach on Sunday evening. Monday morning, I received a phone call from a friend in Bible Study Fellowship (BSF). I had been attending BSF for several years and it had been a great encouragement in my walk with Jesus. I was in a church that was strong in teaching the Word, but not focused so much on application. I loved that BSF was strong in application, and I also loved the small group fellowship. It was a great fit for me. I hung on every word that was said in the small group discussions as well as from our anointed leader. Even the process of joining BSF had been a place of God teaching me the rewards of perseverance and His timing. The waiting list was so long that I had to sign up for the class five times before I was invited to join. As a result of having to wait, Leah was then old enough to go with me and be a part of their wonderful children's program. BSF was another lovely exposure to the greater Body of Christ. I loved the diversity. It was wonderful. It's easy for a local church to focus so much on itself that it can miss the greater Body of Christ. I had served with beautiful believers at the crisis center and now had the privilege of studying the Word and fellowshipping with different believers from many different churches and walks of life.

My friend, Elaine, surprised me with her phone call. She said BSF was going to have a Bible study class in the women's prison and my name had come up as a possible leader. I remember looking up and saying to the Lord, "this is not funny." I wanted to be a pen pal, not go into the prison. However, I knew that God was answering my prayer, so I agreed to meet a few days later for the interview process. One of the requirements of the program was that those in leadership could not have been divorced or married to someone that had been divorced. Since Sam had been married before we met, I was disqualified from being a discussion leader. I was hurt. I felt rejection, but I couldn't be upset with the person who interviewed me because this was not her rule. A couple of weeks passed and I "decided" that somehow I had misunderstood the Lord. However, this was God at work in my life—preparing His right place for me—not disqualifying me. He wanted me to learn to rest in Him and to be willing to wait for His best for me.

I was even more surprised by Elaine's second phone call. She invited me to join the team as the class administrator. The divorce issue would not be a problem with this role. My emotions were still very high and I had no interest in being a part of the class, but I managed to say the right thing. I said I would pray about it. But in my heart I already knew that I would turn her down. In time I would learn that BSF had reasons for their rules. However, I would also learn a more important truth. God is not limited by rules.

The next day Tara had a piano lesson. Leah and I sat in the car doing her Bible study together while we waited. I flipped Leah's devotional book open to the next chapter and we looked up the verses together.

We read: *For I was hungry and you gave me something to eat, I was thirsty and you gave me something to drink, I was a stranger and you invited me in. I needed clothes and you clothed me, I was sick and you looked after me, I was in prison and you came to visit me* (Matthew 25:36).

"Have you ever visited anyone in prison?" Leah asked.

"No."

"Has Daddy?"

"No."

"Well I know that Tara and I haven't," she said before going on to tell me that we needed to find a way to go and visit people in prison. I felt very defensive. I asked her if we had done those other things in this verse. We re-read the list together. In her childlike way, she gave me an example of how we had done each of those other things listed. I couldn't escape God! He had used my own little daughter to speak to me and direct my path.

That night, we prayed together as a family and talked about the invitation to join the BSF prison team. "We" joined the team. I would be the one going in each week, but our whole family would be involved. Many adjustments had to be made by all of us. Tara, at thirteen, took over my role in a children's program at our church on Wednesday nights so I could go to the prison. Because of the shift work that Sam did, our friends would often need to transport our children to church. Tara would have to be responsible for Leah after school because I would need to leave in the afternoon to go to the prison. She would also have to get dinner on the table for the family. We all had to pull together to make it work, therefore it was our family's obedience and endeavor. The decision was not just about me going to be a part of this prison class, it was about our entire family choosing to be obedient even after considering the cost. God was again at work in us!

I thought I was just going to the prison to help inmates. What really happened is that the prison invaded my life and became a huge tool that God would use to direct my life for the next twenty years. As we adapted the Bible Study Fellowship program to the prison, several adjustments had to be made. As the administrator, it was my responsibility to give the introduction class each month for new ladies that were interested in joining. Many of those coming were outside of Christ, had never been in a Bible study, and had trouble reading or understanding the homework lessons. To help with this difficult transition, I not only lead the class the first Wednesday of each month, but also continued to work with that group of ladies for the next three or four weeks until it was time to have another introduction class. This interim process helped us determine which discussion group best fit their abilities as well. I helped them break down the questions and showed them how to find passages in the Word. It was so gratifying for me to be able to help them by simplifying the questions in a way that gave them a better understanding. I had the pleasure of getting to know these ladies and often being the one to lead them to the Lord. I loved watching God use the guidelines, not to restrict me, but to simply move me into a better position of ministry to these precious ladies.

Failures have often been the place of greatest lessons for me. Each year all the BSF leaders began with an area conference at a local retreat center. Sam had been out of work for months recovering from multiple back surgeries. God's direction for our family was to take our needs to Him and not share them with others. It was time for the yearly meeting and we did not have the money for me to cover my expenses. Sam and I prayed and had peace that I was supposed to go and trust Him for provision. When the day came, I still didn't have the needed funds. When the friend I was riding with came to pick me up, all I had in my purse was a handful of change from our coin jar. I fully expected to call Sam that night and have him tell me that we had the money and that I could write a check for my expenses. After dinner, I called home. There was still no money. As evening came, I was becoming more and more uncomfortable because I didn't know what to do. The district leader asked us to settle up our accounts that evening or by first thing the next morning. I went to the leader and explained my situation. She was kind and said she would cover my expense. However, she also questioned me as to whether I should be working instead of serving at the prison. I felt very defeated and was physically sick all night from my frayed nerves. My friend confided in me on the ride home that she had wanted to pay my expenses. In fact, she had tried to pay my bill the night before, but was told it was already paid.

She felt bad that she hadn't shared her plan with me. She assumed I had already paid my own bill. She knew Sam was out of work, and she wanted to bless us. If I had trusted the Lord and waited until the next morning, God would have covered it without me saying a word. That was a powerful and painful lesson for me. The enemy had convinced me that I couldn't go to bed and occupy a room and continue to eat the meals without paying my way first. I should have held firm to God's direction and been expectant for His provision. The lesson I learned in this experience has been invaluable to me many times since then, when it's been the eleventh hour and I haven't yet seen God's provision on the horizon. God doesn't waste anything!

Another important thing God taught me through BSF that has become a foundational block for my life and for ministry is commitment. When we allow ourselves to remember why we are doing something, it helps the gray areas to go away. I am serving for one reason—because God has called me! When He called me, He knew the obstacles I would encounter and factored them into His plans. I don't have the luxury of giving up simply because things are difficult. I'm committed to obey and honor the Lord. My commitment is not to a person; my commitment is to Jesus. This is a great connecting dot to WLFJ. At WLFJ our leadership knows the meaning of commitment. We persevere under lots of difficult circumstances. One of the continuing obstacles that we deal with is the lack of commitment in the Body of Christ. So often a team leader will call or email the day before they are scheduled to come—or even the day of—to tell us they can't come. Many times it's because their team members have changed their minds about coming. There are even those times that teams are scheduled and just don't show up, without any notice. Our dependency is on the Lord to supply what we need. However, we try to never miss the opportunity to address this with those who had planned to serve. There are many times when we have filled our calendar with the maximum number of teams we can take on a particular day such that we actually have to turn others away. Then, on the scheduled day, so many have dropped out at the last minute, we are challenged to serve the community with too few volunteers. This is a chronic problem. The big issue is not whether teams show up to serve at WLFJ or not, but their lack of understanding that our commitment is to Jesus! It is simply a symptom of the great need for deeper intimacy with our amazing God. BSF was an important tool that God used in my life to teach me the value of commitment.

After a couple of years of serving as the administrator and leading the introduction class, a new minimum security prison for women was built in Raleigh. Many of the ladies that attended the BSF prison class were moved to the minimum custody facility. There were no programs there and no chaplain. This first BSF test class for the prison environment had been a very difficult experience. One of the leaders had a child die that year, while other leaders struggled with health and family issues. BSF felt it was too soon to start a program in another prison unit, so the teaching leader and the discussion leaders were asked not to start a Bible study in this new facility. Because I was an administrator, there were no restrictions placed on me. I finished the year as the administrator for BSF, but each night after class I would cross the street to the new facility and lead a Bible study with the ladies that had been moved. The next year I stepped aside from BSF and only taught this new and growing class. I learned a very important lesson. Our God is a Sovereign God; that is a fact revealed to us in scripture. However, allowing its application to work in my life was another thing. The more I learned to rest in His sovereignty, the less I was tossed around by my circumstances and emotions. He loves me. His plans for me can't be messed up by someone else or something outside of my control. He's the One with control. This was becoming a place I could run to for stability in my life. When the circumstances around me seemed huge and looming, He was teaching me to go back to the place that was in control—Him and His sovereignty over all. This became a continual learning curve for me. He's so good to keep working with us as He gently presses us to Himself.

God taught me that He is able to work through human rules

to accomplish His purposes. He never makes a mistake and is never surprised or limited by the circumstances of life. His plans and his purposes prevail. It was His purpose for me to lead this new class. He used my obedience and my submission to the authority over me not only to accomplish His plan and His purposes for me, but also for His plan and purposes for these dear ladies. My call to the prison was very clear. God had spoken and I was committed to obey. He worked through that to open a door for me that would have otherwise been closed. I was the most unlikely person in my eyes to lead this new class, but I was His choice. He was not limited by me or my inability. It was His plan and His class. Our family was stepping into a new threshold of blessing, challenge, and adventure. BSF was an amazing tool of growth in my life. I learned so much. Those in charge would soon make the decision to no longer have a BSF prison class, but not before they laid the beautiful ground work for me to begin this new ministry. The class in the maximum security unit continued with a local church taking over, so the efforts and ground work of BSF blessed both prisons. I'm confident that BSF originally thought they were starting a new arm of their ministry, but God was using their efforts as His tool for His purposes. It was all good! When God says something or makes a promise, it will happen. Often it's not the way we expect because we process it through our earthly lenses, but it's His Word and He will carry it out. God had me in His school. He was teaching me so much for the future. I had needed to learn the importance of submission to authority in order to better understand His ability to work in all situations to accomplish His purposes. God's plan prevailed!

God gave our family unusual favor at the prison. The superintendent at the new prison had no programs and no help. She soon realized that the ladies attending Wednesday night Bible study were some of the best behaved and most cooperative of all the residents. I often took Tara and Leah with me to the prison. The ladies who were separated from their own children loved when my girls came with me. Their own families were not allowed to visit them on Christmas for security reasons, but my family had clearance. We spent most Christmas Eves at the prison with these dear ladies. With the help of a great team, we prepared shopping bags of hygiene items, books, a new towel or a needed clothing item, and homemade Christmas goodies. The ladies were so blessed by these simple acts of kindness. Also, once a month, we prepared a special dessert for ladies attending Bible study. Those were the nights we had the largest crowds. Some of the regular attendees felt offended that people came just for dessert night, but we were delighted. Just like the little children in the Bible Club years earlier that came for cookies and left with Jesus, and our honored guests at WLFJ that come for the food and leave with Jesus, many of these ladies came to know Jesus because they showed up to have a piece of homemade pie or brownies. We were walking God's unseen, but very real, path.

As our favor with the prison continued to grow, we organized a team of volunteers who received special clearance to take residents of the prison out to church on Sunday, or to one of their homes for an evening meal away from the prison. We had great opportunities to disciple the ladies from the Bible study who were so new in the Lord. If an inmate had a death in her family or a family crisis, I would often get a phone call from the prison superintendent asking if I could take the inmate to visit her family or to a funeral or a hospital visit. For the prison, it was a help to not have to send staff, and for the resident, it was a blessing to not have to be escorted by an officer. The superintendent realized that the ladies in the Bible study were getting good support and help. She would often share her concerns with me regarding the stress that the staff and officers lived with daily as a result of working in such a difficult place. There were times when she would call me in and ask if I could help with someone on staff who was struggling or had emotional needs. Sometimes the employees at the prison would come to me on their own to share their need for prayer. It was wonderful to watch God at work in so many different ways.

On occasion, we planned movie nights in our home and brought the ladies out for an evening of pizza, popcorn, and the freedom of being away from the prison for a while. The prison officials never worried that the ladies out with our team might be involved in something they shouldn't be doing. We built great relationships with the inmates, but also with the prison guards and administrators. It was an unusual opportunity. We didn't realize at the time what a privilege we had been given. One of the sweet memories for our family came years later when Tara got married. I brought five ladies from the prison to our home to make cookies, cheese straws, sausage balls, bird seed bags, and other wedding essentials. We spent an entire Saturday cooking, freezing, and preparing for Tara's big event. When the time arrived, the ladies were then allowed to come to the wedding. It was a great blessing for our family and a special event for these sisters in Christ who had never been exposed to a Christian wedding. All the leftovers, including cake and other goodies, were carefully packaged and taken to the prison the next Wednesday night for the ladies who were not able to attend. There were dear ladies in that class years ago who are still friends of our family today.

Something else very surprising happened to me a few years into leading this class that forever changed me; something that God would use to impact the ladies attending the class. My routine each day was to get lunch for my girls, and then they were required to rest on their beds and either nap or read for an hour. They needed this slow-down time, but I also needed the break. I would get them settled down and then I'd turn on *Focus on the Family* and listen to the wonderful guest speakers that Dr. Dobson had on each day.

On this particular day, I was folding laundry at the dining room table when the Lord spoke to my heart. He said, "Sit down at the table. This program is for you." There was a nervousness that came over me as I seated myself at the table and continued to fold the clothes. The speaker was Rich Buhler who had written a book entitled *Pain and Pretending*. He was a counselor and was sharing about his practice dealing with victims of abuse. As he began to talk, I realized that he was describing me in great detail. Tears poured down my face as I realized for the first time why I struggled in so many areas of my life. My constant battle with overeating, insecurity in relationships, fear of being noticed or having attention drawn to me, and the anxiety over the safety of my children began to make sense to me. Very gently God pulled back a curtain and allowed me to see and "remember" things that had been blocked out of my mind. One of the things that Buhler said was that if you are dealing with these things you might be tempted to try to deal with it alone with God, but you will not be able to. He strongly advised getting help.

God connected me with a wonderful Christian counselor who worked with me over the next year. Debbie allowed me to pay whatever I could afford, and she met with me regularly. The mountain of my past was huge, and the work to get through it appeared to never end. It was the most painful year of my life. I felt like I cried all the time. God was unearthing so much from my childhood so I could forever be freed from it. I felt like I had to re-learn everything. I didn't know what was normal. Everything I did, it seemed, had to be examined. My mind was riddled with unhealthy thinking. When a child is abused, there is a branding that takes place, one which requires help and time to erase. My self-worth had been destroyed to the point that I reacted to nearly every situation in life with an overwhelming need to prove I had value. At the same time, I felt labeled as different from other people—not normal. The abusers had taken from me any ability to feel safe. God had to invade all of the places and feelings that were damaged with His Word and healing touch. I always tried to protect myself and had to learn how to trust God to be my protector. God used Debbie to chip away the shell I had built around myself so His healing balm could penetrate my life.

One morning as I sat with God, He gave me a verse that I would hang on to during that year and thereafter. *But whenever anyone turns to the Lord, the veil is taken away. Now the Lord is the Spirit, and where the Spirit of the Lord is, there is freedom* (2 Corinthians 3:16-17, NIV). That's exactly what God did. He pulled back a veil and allowed me to see what I had not remembered, and then He brought healing and freedom. The year with my counselor and friend Debbie became not only another step of great healing in my life, but also a time of God fanning into flame His gift within me.

The Lord gave me amazing "God appointments" for years to come. I became sensitized to those around me who had suffered abuse. Often when someone behaved badly or had an unusual reaction to a situation, God would help me to see the buried pain that prompted this response. At the crisis center, in the prison, at WLFJ, and in daily life, His heart of compassion rose up in me when I encountered the evidence of pain in a young woman's life. The place that was so painful in my life was redeemed by God and used for ministry. The time came when I thanked God for this deep and painful abuse, because He was using it for good, far outweighing the harm it had inflicted. We have an amazing, loving God. Out of the storehouses of our sin, mistakes, and the wrongs committed against us come beautiful Kingdom treasures. Much of the community that we serve at WLFJ comes from generational pain, coupled with the pain of their own individual choices. Most have no idea that life can be different for them. They have no idea of the power and redemptive ability of our God. It is wonderful to be able to give hope to the hopeless.

As a young girl reared in a mixed up family, I dreamed of being a social worker. When it was time to go to college, my parents paid for me to go to a year of business school. After business school, I went to work and college never happened. But God is the Sovereign God and His purposes always prevail. He has given me an incredible education through the school of life. God's path of healing is unique for each of His children. My healing—and my equipping to help others—has been a process of God using many different people. Most often it came through new places where God called me into ministry. The training I took with the crisis center was a piece of that puzzle, and my time with Debbie was another. The prison, people, ministries, and books have all had their place. It has been like the peeling of an onion, one layer at a time. The refining and healing process continues, and I have learned to rejoice in God's perfect process for me. As I met with Debbie, God helped me to see places where my "belief system" was wrong. He helped me to know how to establish a new and healthy one built on truth. At the crisis center and the prison, God placed within me a love for young women who felt their lives were forever ruined.

We, as the Body of Christ, throw around terms like "codependency" and "dysfunction." We label ourselves and others by our failures, frailties, and deficiencies. We compare ourselves with others in order to determine our shortages or superiorities, both of which are Satan's tools. God looks at our brokenness, and He sees an opportunity for usefulness. As we read the Word, we clearly see that God chose to use the misfits, the broken, the misunderstood, and the great places of lack to reveal His power and His greatness. It was not by accident or chance that God chose to work through people like Tamar, Ruth, David, Abraham, and Peter. It was His choice and good pleasure. The closer we grow in our walk with Him, the more we yearn for wholeness because we want our love and dependency to be in Him and not in things or people. We often allow ourselves to focus on our need for healing when we should strive for intimacy with Him. God can be trusted to direct our healing and our path to wholeness. This work in us will continue until we see Him face to face.

I can remember sitting in church during the days of working through the abuse and wanting desperately to worship the Lord. Tears would course down my cheeks as I tried to focus on the Lord instead of the raging thoughts running through my mind. My eyes saw the others around me worshipping with what appeared to be ease while I felt so condemned. God helped me to understand that my striving to worship Him in the midst of my pain was huge in His sight. I had lived too many years trusting and believing that my feelings revealed truth. In reality, what I chose to do was much greater than how I felt. I chose to go to church no matter how I felt. I chose to focus on Jesus and His gift of salvation to me no matter how I felt. I chose to believe He would get me to the other side no matter how I felt. He understood because Jesus went to the cross despising the shame, but looking ahead to what His sacrifice would accomplish. He understood that obedience without good feelings was honoring the Father. He helped me to understand that what felt to me like being phony, was in reality living a life that honored Him. I chose truth. I chose to believe Him regardless of how I felt. This was His training ground to teach me to walk in reality. This was not being phony!

I also learned in this painful process that the more I acted on truth instead of feelings, the more those feelings began to change. Knowing the truth, choosing to act on that truth and making it my focus—instead of how I felt—brought my crazy, out of control feelings into line with the truth of God's Word. The feelings were the last to change, but they did change. This too was a step of faith. This obedience lead to deeper intimacy with God.

I grew and thrived as I continued to walk out my own healing with Him, and as God gave me opportunities to share the healing truth of His principles with others. God met me in my place of struggle with His sweet promises and words of encouragement. One morning, as I thought about the young girl who was injured and the childhood that was a mess, God gave me His encouragement. The Israelites who had seen the original temple were struggling as they compared it to the rebuilt one. The glory of the former seemed so much greater than the present one. *The glory of this present house will be greater than the glory of the former house, says the Lord Almighty. And in this place I will grant peace, declares the Lord Almighty* (Haggai 2:9, NIV). God encouraged me that the pretty, innocent little girl that had been hurt was being rebuilt into a place of greater glory. His presence made my rebuilt life more beautiful than the former, and in this redeemed life there is peace. Debbie once used the helpful illustration that in the light of eternity, a lost childhood was like the loss of two hundred dollars to a millionaire. For me, it was definitely a loss, but couldn't compare to all that I now had in Christ. Eternity and a never-ending life with Jesus became my new focus.

The Lord was at work healing and restoring me as I continued to teach the prison Bible study. I'd cry all the way to class each week, arguing with the Lord and asking Him why He was sending *me* to these hurting ladies. I was a total mess. How did I expect to help them? I couldn't even help myself. I pleaded with the Lord to send them a real teacher and to let me have time to deal with myself. What I later learned is that going to the prison was for my healing. The ladies simply received the overflow. The truths that God taught me each week were turned into worksheets that I used for the Bible study for the prisoners. Yes, they were in a physical prison, but many who appear to walk freely around planet earth are in more confining prisons. These ladies were learning who they were in Christ and walking in freedom from addiction and childhood abuse. They were also learning to accept responsibility for their own sins and failures. Many living outside prison walls have no idea of the depth of the prison walls around them.

The ladies in the prison class studied the Bible together not just for education and head knowledge but for growth, application, and freedom. Together, we came to worship the Lord and get to know Him better. He became their freedom. I would say to them, "it's more important to put into practice what you know than to learn more just for the sake of knowing." These persevering ladies became great truth walkers. We would say together, "I feel____"(like a failure, hopeless, unloved — whatever), "but the truth is___"(I am a child of God, I am loved, I am victorious, I have a hope and a future). As they studied the Word each week, I had them highlight what the Word said about them. We talked about it the next week. We came to believe it and to live it. Like me, so many of these ladies had spent their entire lives feeling accepted or, more often rejected, by their performance. The release that we all experienced as we meditated on, repeated together, and prayed through the beautiful truths of our identity, because of what Christ had done for us, was incredible. We asked Holy Spirit God to make it reality in our lives. The class grew from a handful in the first weeks to eighty or more at different times. This small prison only housed about two hundred and fifty ladies, so God's Word was impacting a large percentage of the population.

One sweet lady stands out to me. Rita came to class each week but never sang the songs during our worship time. She would somewhat do her homework but stayed a little aloof from the rest of the class. I looked for ways to make conversation with her and she'd be responsive but not engaging. She never gave a prayer request and I knew nothing about her. This went on for months while we talked about our identity in Christ weekly. One truth that the ladies loved was that we are saints. Some were from Catholic backgrounds, so this seemed very strange but intriguing to them. Week after week, as we talked about who we are in Christ, someone always brought up that we are saints. One night Rita came to class and on her name tag, she had written "Saint Rita." From that day on she smiled, sang, interacted with the class discussion, did her homework, and allowed me into her life. What fun it was to watch God make His Word reality in the lives of these ladies!

While serving at the prison, our family continued to take ladies to live with us from the crisis center. Most came for only a few weeks, not long term. God burdened my heart for the ladies in the prison class who were being released back to families that were often the reason they were in trouble in the first place. God often took me to Isaiah 58 and caused it to come alive to me. *Your people will rebuild…you will be called Repairer of Broken Walls, Restorer of Streets with dwellings…if you spend yourself in behalf of the hungry and satisfy the needs of the oppressed, then your light will rise in the darkness, and your night will become like the noonday. The Lord will guide you always; he will satisfy your needs in a sun-scorched land and will strengthen your frame. You will be like a well-watered garden, like a spring whose waters never fail…share your food with the hungry, provide the poor wanderer with shelter, loose the chains of injustice…"* I could not shake it. God was working His plan for our family. It was exciting, exhilarating, daunting, but unmistakably His unfolding plan.

So one day "I decided" that God was calling me to start an aftercare ministry. My pastor friend, Larry, and his wife, Mary, had a heart for the hurting. They had been neighbors in one of our first apartments as new believers. Larry was attending seminary at the time and Mary's hands were full with their active little boys. We had shared many times of fellowship and had grown in the Lord together. I went to them to talk to them about opening their home to ladies coming out of prison. God had just moved them into a large older home that they knew would be for ministry. They were the perfect family. After all, he was a preacher. This had to be what God was saying to me. My family was not the right place, nor were we equipped spiritually, emotionally, or economically. Mary and Larry opened their home and we began to work together for them to take ladies who needed a place to live once they were released. We were in ministry at the crisis center together, and they often welcomed those ladies into their home as well. For some time, it went well, but soon we realized this was not to continue.

Even in our messes, God is at work. Tammy attended the prison class and she was one of those lovely places where God was at work. We had already prepared a room in Mary and Larry's home to house a lady from the prison. We had one particular person in mind, but had no idea when she would be released. We soon came to realize that God had His own plan. One morning Tammy woke up in her prison cell to hear God say it was time to pack up her things. She was leaving the prison that day. The other inmates and the officers laughed at her because no paperwork had been received and there had been no word from the prison administrator indicating that she was going to leave. But, Tammy had a word from the Lord. She packed her few personal things and sat on her bed waiting for the prison to catch up with God. Just before dinner, an administrator came to her cell in the maximum-custody unit and told her she was free to leave. They allowed her to call me. I stopped in front of the prison gate and she hopped into my car. God had not only delivered her, but had also prepared a place for her to go.

Tammy was difficult to deal with at times. Yes, she knew the Lord, but she also had a strong personality and a heavy-duty past. She lived with Mary and Larry's family for several months before getting on her feet and moving on to the next step of life. I often had to say something to Tammy about her attitude. One day she exploded in exasperation and said, "What is attitude?" I realized that for weeks I had been addressing something, but she had no idea what I meant. As I explained to her that her bad moods and careless, hurtful words were her bad attitude, she laughed and said, "I'm always like this. This is who I am." We saw Holy Spirit God peel away one layer and begin to build an understanding of her identity in Christ. As God had taught me, He allowed me to pass it on to Tammy.

For Mary, Larry, and me, the aftercare ministry became a teaching and learning experience that we would all benefit from greatly in the future. In the years to come, I continued to struggle with how it was possible that God had called our family to care for people in our home. All I could see was our dysfunction and lack. How could we be a family for hurting people to look to as a good example? What did we have to offer anyone? It is interesting how we can easily see others need to grow in the Lord and often miss our own. I was on God's training ground, learning my own identity in Christ. In time I learned that our lack becomes our equipping. We were totally dependent on the Lord. Apart from Him we had nothing to offer others. Even our many mistakes would give others hope that they too could make it. God had already factored in my failure and was going to use it. He had a plan. God encouraged and comforted me through His Word.

In Genesis 18, God came to Abraham and shared His plan to destroy Sodom and Gomorrah. Abraham pleaded with God for the safety of his nephew Lot. Over and again Abraham seemed to be negotiating with God for the protection of his family. Abraham finally asked God if He would spare Sodom and Gomorrah if he found ten righteous people there. God agreed. God knew Abraham's heart was for Lot and his family. Genesis 19:27 gives us Abraham's view as he walked out of his tent the next morning and faced toward Sodom and Gomorrah to see smoke rising across the horizon. We are never told in scripture if Abraham knew that God spared Lot's life. Abraham looked out and saw the evidence of destruction and must have assumed that Lot was dead. Abraham, in his pain and not understanding God's ways, packed up his camp and moved. I'm sure he did not want to look in that direction and face this painful view each morning. I can't help wondering if part of his pain was remembering that God's original word to him was to leave his family behind when he moved (Genesis 12). God had specifically said to leave his home and his family, yet Abraham had not fully obeyed. He left most of his family, but took his nephew Lot with him. Now in Abraham's mind, Lot was dead. Abraham's emotions were probably a mixture of his own guilt and anger with God. The spiral of his emotions affected his behavior (Genesis 20). He repeated a sin by lying about Sarah to protect himself. He told Abimelech that she was his sister instead of his wife. God stepped into Abraham's mess and protected Sarah by speaking to Abimelech in a dream. Abimelech was instructed to return Sarah to Abraham. God called Abraham His prophet and told Abimelech that Abraham would pray for him and he would live. God's protection was all over Abraham and Sarah. In the midst of Abraham's mess, God set him up for blessing. God knew that Abraham was reeling in pain and lack of understanding, but God's relationship with Abraham was intact. Abraham was on God's training ground and He was not shocked or surprised by Abraham's behavior.

I heard God's call to care for people, but I assumed, based on my perception of me, that God could not use me, so I had put the burden on Mary and Larry. I was wrong, yet God still blessed. I learned that it's wrong to draw a conclusion from facts—or what appear to be the facts—without going to God for His truth. Abraham came to a wrong conclusion and acted unwisely. Later in Genesis, when Jacob was given the evidence of a blood-stained robe, he didn't go to the Lord for the truth, but trusted the story he was given and jumped to his own conclusions. (Genesis 37). He spent many years grieving for the loss of his son, Joseph, who was very much alive. Many years later, Joshua looked at the evidence produced by the Gibeonites—their worn out clothes, the moldy bread, mended wineskins—and believed their lie without seeking God. This resulted in him making an unwise decision.

God wants me to look at the information given—the facts—and ask Him for the truth. We are called to walk the truth and not the facts. I was so thankful for the comfort of the Word! My relationship with the Lord was secure. I was not a failure or a disappointment to Him. I was on His training ground. He is a great redeemer. The facts for me were that I couldn't do it. I couldn't help ladies coming out of prison. I couldn't make a difference in their lives. I thought I was totally inadequate for what God was calling me to do, but the truth was that God was covering my lack with His perfect wisdom and provision. I didn't have to be able, I just had to be willing and obedient as God continued to teach me to look at the facts given to me, but take those facts to Him, and get His view before moving ahead with a decision. God's ways are different from the ways of this world. We need His continued focus to partner with Holy Spirit God in doing His work.

This lesson has been another place of connecting dots to the work God is doing at WLFJ. A fire marshal's report, a threat from our former landlord, or a financial crisis can quickly serve up the temptation to believe that we will either be closed down or forced to move. Emotions can quickly rise when looking at the facts, until Holy Spirit God gently reminds us to take the facts to the Lord and get His Word before making a decision. The length of time I focus on the facts before running to the Lord dictates how long I will battle with the negative emotions. God is merciful to continue to work with me. It's hard and doesn't always make sense to us, but we are called to walk truth—not facts.

As the prison ministry grew, I had to step aside from the crisis center. The center had approached me about a staff position with them. I wanted that position, but it was Tara's last year in high school. God showed me that this was an important time in her life for me to be at home. I felt that we needed the income, but I had been called first and foremost to my family, and I didn't need to allow myself to get too busy elsewhere. Many of Tara's friends were from families where both parents worked. After school our house became the gathering place for school projects, homework, snacks, and fun. Some of Tara's friends came to know the Lord. They saw a family life different from what they were living and many seeds were planted in their young lives. There was often an extra one or two at the dinner table at night. Tara said to me one day, "Mom, we are the only family I know that eats dinner together." It didn't seem to matter to those around the table if it was potato soup, or eggs with rice, or a chicken casserole. They seemed to enjoy our farmhouse dwelling which paled in comparison to most of their houses. These times around the table became increasingly more important to me, and I saw again that *"your wife will be like a fruitful vine within your house"* was about more than just our family.

Tara got her license and began to drive our only car. I would stand at the door and pray as she pulled out of our driveway. I asked Sam if he thought I'd ever quitting doing that. He said he hoped not. I was upset with myself because my concern was more about whether the car would be safe than Tara. I asked the Lord to help me understand this strange thinking of mine. He told me that I had given Him Tara many years earlier, but I had never given Him the car. I could almost hear God chuckle as He told me that. My response was that I could fix that right away. That day, I gave Him the car and never had that concern again, but I did still keep praying over car and driver!

Tara wanted her own car, but knew we couldn't buy her one. We prayed together about it each night and asked the Lord to provide a car for her when He knew she was ready to have one. One day we came home to find a car parked in our driveway. The title and key was tucked in the front door, along with a note from a friend. We had helped this friend years earlier when she and her husband were struggling with a past-due power bill. God had blessed them with a new car, and when they thought about selling their old one, God reminded them of our family. They knew Tara was driving and that we had people living in our home who needed to be driven from place to place, so they decided to give the car to our family. Tara drove that car until she left home for college. It was a bit of a clunker but it was a good little car for her.

Two years later, Tara headed off for what we thought would

be her first year of college toward a four-year degree. Instead, it became a year of learning to live on her own in preparation for a different career. She and her boyfriend, Greg, became engaged. At nineteen, she was a wife and living on the west coast, and I felt like such a failure as a mom. We loved Greg and knew that this was the right time for their life together to begin, but I grieved over her leaving so young. I told the Lord that there was more I wanted to teach her. This step in her life seemed to happen too soon. I felt like my own time of healing had stolen away time from Tara. God was good to comfort me. He told me to pray that there would be godly women in her life who would continue the discipleship that she needed, and for me to look for someone to sow into as well. God gave us a fun and unexpected answer to that prayer. Tara's best friend, Tonia, was working and wanted to go to cosmetology school, but couldn't afford to support herself while attending school. Like Tara, Tonia needed discipleship and a godly woman in her life. She was already like family, so she moved in with us. She was someone for Leah to enjoy, someone that we as a family were comfortable with, and someone who needed our family. She was a perfect fit for this time in our lives.

Sam's makeup and gifting is not such that you would likely see him leading a small group or a Bible study. He's not inclined to stand up in church and share, but he is a gentle giant. He has been used by God to reveal a father's love to our daughters, as well as many other young women over the years who have lived in our home. There's no better preparation to accept the love of Father God than to have the sacrificial, protective, unconditional love of an earthly father. Sam's love and compassion is packaged in a rugged exterior, but those who know him well and those who lived in our home have experienced this gift. He has big, strong hands that have cross stitched with his daughters, repaired broken jewelry, fixed broken cars, and given great back rubs. I can still see Sam sitting on the sofa watching TV with Tonia, soaking his big hands in some solution as she was giving him a manicure for her homework assignment. Sam took her out like he took our girls out. We all received her experimental haircuts and survived. Tonia is forever an extension of our family.

God did provide a lovely group of ladies in Bremerton, Washington who took my Tara under their wings and loved and mentored her. Greg was in the Navy, on the USS Nimitz, and away much of the time. These ladies became family to Tara. I desperately wanted to be the one to be in Tara's life because I was her mom and felt it was my right. The Lord helped me see that my heart should be more focused on her need than on my rights. This became another opportunity for me to surrender to His plan. Tara called me once each week and I called her once a week as well. In this way, we shared the expense of talking regularly. There were no cell phones in those days, but we wrote lots of letters. One night, she called me late in the evening. She had awoken to a noise at her door and was frightened. We were more than three thousand miles apart and there was nothing I could do but pray. We prayed together, then I told her to hang up the phone, call her neighbor, and ask him to walk to her door and check it out for her. After she called him, she called me back. We stayed on the phone until he arrived, and I was sure Tara was safe. This was such a hopeless and helpless feeling for me. My daughter was in crisis and I was too far away to do any-thing—but together we prayed and trusted God and He provid-ed. I reminded her of the Psalm God had given her when He called her to be Greg's wife and move to the other side of the world from me. We read some of those verses together. *I will say of the Lord, 'He is my refuge and my fortress, my God in whom I trust.' Surely he will save you from the fowler's snare and from the deadly pestilence. He will cover you with his feathers, and under his wings you will find refuge...You will not fear the terror of night...A thousand may fall at your side, ten thousand at your right hand, but it will not come near you...no harm will befall you, no disaster will come near your tent. For he will command his angels concerning you to guard you in all your ways...* (Psalm 91).

Even as God had called another group of ladies to minister to Tara, He also gave me special times as well. My opportunities to influence and encourage her were not over. They were simply different. The Lord carried me down a road of surrender to His plan for their lives. I knew Tara and Greg had a heart for ministry and assumed they would one day be on the mission field somewhere. They lived 3,013 miles from us, and I had to come to the realization that I would probably never be in my grandchildren's lives on a regular basis. I decided ahead of time that I would be the best long-distant grandmother in the world. We suspected that Greg might make the Navy a career. I knew that God called me to surrender my desire to His and leave my children and grandchildren (yet unborn) to Him.

When Tara called to tell us she was pregnant, I wanted to go see her and help out when the baby came but there was no money for such a trip. I was homeschooling Leah, so she would need to go, too. We decided to put aside whatever money we could and ask God to bless our little savings. Leah and I collected cans, did a weekly paper route, and looked for every way to put aside any extra money. We sold one of our cars and put that money aside, then added that year's tax refund to it as well. Tara wanted me to come visit her for her baby shower. Also, Greg was going to be out to sea about the time the baby was due, so she wanted me and Leah to come and stay with her during that time so she wouldn't be alone. We wanted Sam to be able to come, too. All together we needed to save for four roundtrip tickets — two for me and one each for Sam and Leah. We had only saved enough for two tickets and Tara's shower was approaching. The airlines ran an unexpected offer for flights from Charlotte to Bremerton; two for the price of one for a small window of time. We rushed to the airlines with our money and purchased four tickets. We were so excited. Our frequent flyer miles earned during this time gave us the ability to purchase one more ticket. When the baby was a few months old, and Greg was on a long duty out to sea, Tara and the baby would be able to fly home to stay with us during those months. We were beside ourselves with joy. I had my visit with Tara for a week to attend her shower, meet her friends, and help get the nursery ready. Then, Leah and I flew out about a week before Aaron was due and stayed with her for eight weeks. Leah was in her last year of middle school. Our plan was to start her in public school that year, but this changed our plans. It was a wonderful time together and offered lots of dimensions to Leah's education. Sam was able to take his vacation and join us for two of those weeks. We were amazed at God's multiplication. We had saved for two tickets and God gave us five for our money! God doesn't add. He multiplies!

Chapter 6
Learning God's Heart for Unity

Who are those who fear the Lord?
He will show them the path they should choose.
Psalm 25:12, NLT

Another thing God is helping me to learn is the importance of declaring truth with my words. We have to be so careful with what comes out of our mouths. The same mouth can go from speaking blessings to speaking curses. Words are powerful. We speak many words every day, so God helped me to see how important it is to use my words to partner with His truth. As I looked around at the events of life, it was easy to focus on circumstances. God has taught me to focus instead on what He is doing. As I had taught the ladies in the prison, God would have me say "the fact is___(we don't have money to pay this bill, or this situation seems hopeless, or whatever the fact or circumstance might be), but "the truth is God is at work (or God has promised, or God's Word says) and I am expectant to see Him be glorified in this and for me be blessed."

This exercise diffuses the enemy and gets my mind in the

right place. Jesus wants me to know the truth of His Word and His greatness and focus on Him. He called me to see my brothers and sisters in Christ as saints, holy, set apart by God, and not focus on any behavior that did not line up with that. As I struggled with strongholds, habits, and difficulties in my own life, I said over and over, "I will not give up. God is at work in this. Victory is mine!" The temptation was to declare the opposite, but God was, and is, strengthening me. He wants me to walk daily in the truth that I can do all that He has called me to do because Christ is strengthening and equipping me and the victory is mine. He died and rose so I could have it. I usually have a list in my Bible of the current things that I need to declare and proclaim. He has taught me that these declarations along with prayer are often the only way I can partner with Him in what He is doing in my life or the life of someone else.

* * *

Back when we first moved into our "farmhouse," Leah was confused when she found out that Mr. Clyde lived in close walking distance to us. Mr. Clyde was a helper in the children's program in our church. In Leah's mind, he was supposed to live at church because that's where Leah always saw him. She loved him! It took Leah a while to process it, but she soon loved the idea that we could see him often and not just at church. Mr. Clyde was a widower and loved children. He was much older than Sam and me and had known the Lord much longer. He was retired and his children were grown, but kept himself busy with a big yard and a big house. Sometimes when he was working in the yard, Leah would ask to go visit. In the winter, we would call and ask if it was a good time to come for a visit. We'd sit by his wood stove and chat. There were many days that I would notice Mr. Clyde working in his yard, and I would walk over and talk. He would do the same. We would often pray together. He was a very good friend to our family. His father became an invalid and lived with him for a short time before passing away. Tara would often sit with Mr. Clyde's father for a few hours so that he could grocery shop or do errands. When Tara got married, Mr. Clyde blessed our family in so many practical ways and even gave me the money to buy my mother of the bride dress. Leah was three when we moved close to him. We lived there until Leah graduated from high school.

I guess I knew we were a bit odd as a family. We didn't fit into a normal mold. People had a hard time figuring us out. Not only did we have strangers living with us, but I didn't work outside our home when we could have definitely used more income. Instead of working I was involved in taking a stand against abortion and teaching at the prison. Tara was in public school, yet we homeschooled Leah. That made no sense to others. Sam's job required him to work a different shift every week, so our lives were geared around that constant change. We were different, and it seemed that we were getting *more* different as time went on.

A new family joined our church. John and Joan, with their three daughters, moved from Maine where they had attended a church similar to ours. John served as a leader in the church and took a great interest in our odd family. He was a gifted Bible teacher, and began to shoulder some of the pastoral responsibilities in our church. He started a monthly Bible study at the men's prison and Sam joined his team. Joan was good with children and served in children's ministry. In time, she joined my team at the women's prison. I began to talk with them about the desire God had given us to share our home with ladies coming out of prison and they were encouraging. One of the situations that we would need to consider was that many of the ladies in the prison had children that they had been away from for some time. Once they were released, it was important to them to have their children back as soon as possible. Many of the ladies needed time to get a job and get on their feet before they could handle the additional responsibility of parenting their children alone. Our house had a spacious attic with a permanent stairway. Over the years we had moved the owner's things to one part of the attic and it was a fun place for our girls to play. They had many adventures in that attic. We considered asking our landlord if he would allow us to enclose part of that attic to create another room.

As we were thinking and praying through all these things, I invited Mr. Clyde to lunch one Sunday after church. He had always listened with interest when I shared about the prison class. When Laura lived us, and later when Tonia lived with us, he had seemed supportive. But, he became very quiet and unresponsive at lunch as we shared with him our thoughts about possible aftercare for some of the ladies from the prison. I was not sure exactly what, but realized that something I had said wasn't settling well with him. The next day I called him to try to better understand our odd interaction at lunch. He told me that he was fearful and anxious about a prisoner living so close to him. I listened and tried to respond to his concerns, but he remained troubled. We prayed together, but I knew he was still uneasy.

The following day we received a phone call from one of the men in leadership at the church who wanted us to come to a meeting. Sam had to work, but I went. Mr. Clyde had called his daughter, who also attended our church, and she called the leadership, fearful for her dad's safety. The church leadership told us that we could not take prisoners into our home. We were totally surprised by this decision. We tried to understand and even to defend our position, but there was no ability to reason with anyone. I tried to explain that these ladies were sisters in Christ—not prisoners. We would never take someone into our home to live with our children who was not safe. Some of the ladies that had already lived with us had come to us not yet saved. These dear ladies from the prison knew the Lord and wanted to walk with Him and honor Him with their lives. There were no words that could be said that would help them understand. I couldn't make sense of any of this confusion.

God comforted me during these days. He helped me understand that our brothers and sisters in Christ were struggling with their own identities in Christ. If we realize the place we hold in our position in Christ Jesus, it's much easier for us to also see others in the same way. If we struggle with our past and our own place of acceptance, we have trouble accepting others as new creations in Christ. I needed to rest in Him and His sovereignty. We are all on a different training ground with the Lord. He teaches each of us personally. There are times when a truth becomes reality to me and someone else cannot understand it. There are plenty of times when God is working in someone else yet it isn't a place I can relate. God had been teaching me to live my life and view others from the position of our identity in Christ. As God worked with me, I also needed to rest in His work in others. Despite feeling helpless and stunned, I knew His plan would rise up out of all this. I tried to figure out how to go back and undo this problem and start over. It was impossible.

Sam and I met with John and Joan to see if they had any insights to help us. John visited Mr. Clyde and tried to minister to him, but he could not be consoled. John talked with Mr. Clyde's daughter. She, too, was not able to understand why anyone would want to do such a seemingly foolish thing as having prisoners live with them. The four of us were surprised by the severe reaction of all those around us. Sam and I prayed about our next step. We knew what God had said to us. We also knew that He had placed us in this church, so there had to be a solution. God had clearly directed us to this church. He had not called us to leave. We felt caught between what God had said to us and our church family. Two days later, we received a phone call from our landlord telling us that if we took prisoners into our home, he would make us move. Mr. Clyde and his daughter had called him (they knew him from years earlier when he was their neighbor). He was worried for Mr. Clyde and his family. Their concerns were a heavy burden on him. We apologized for getting him involved in this situation. In all the years we had lived there, we'd never had any negative communication with him. He loved having us in his house, and would stop by to visit whenever he was in town. We were shocked and sad for the way our family seemed to be *turning the world upside down.*

My frustration was great. I wanted to be understood. I wanted my church family to be supportive of this place that God had led us. I wrestled with the Lord through these days, not understanding how His direction to us could be so clear—but only clear to us. We knew the enemy was in the middle of this, trying to divide and destroy, but we also knew the greater truth—God had a plan. These brothers and sisters in Christ loved us and we loved them. We knew their hearts were not against us. We cried out to the Lord for resolution. How could this be happening?

What were we to do? John and Joan started helping us as we looked for another place to live. Nothing was in our price range. God answered our cry by giving us very clear direction. He said we were going to move, but the time was not right. Our position was to wait and watch Him work. In the meantime, my friend Amy, who was the director of a local maternity home, called me. She and I had worked together to help young women in crisis pregnancies when I was serving at the crisis center. We had become good friends. A young woman that she was working with at the maternity home had decided to parent her little girl instead of placing her for adoption. Her daughter was now three and the mom was still struggling to have victory over addictions in her life. She wanted to walk with the Lord, but was a mess. Amy asked if I would call on her and try to encourage her.

I began to meet with Sarah once a week to pray with her and try to give her some accountability. She was a beautiful young woman, the same age of my Tara (who was then living in the state of Washington). My heart broke for Sarah as I watched her great desire to do right, and yet her total inability to make it. Her daughter, Jill, was a smart child but was suffering under the unstable home life. Sam, Leah, and I prayed. We called Tara and Greg and asked them to pray with us. We processed the truth that what makes someone a prisoner is the absence of freedom and not where they live. Sarah was definitely a prisoner, though she had never been incarcerated. We realized Sarah was our first prisoner. After several months of working with her, we invited Sarah and Jill to move in with us. We were not bucking the authority of our church leaders or our landlord because she was not what they labeled a prisoner. We talked with John and Joan about it. We all had peace that this was the direction we should go. God had given His solution. Again, He had called us to submit to the authority as He revealed our next step to stay on His unseen path. Sometimes when God takes us over similar ground numerous times, it's because we didn't get it the first time. Other times it's because He is taking us to a new level of understanding.

For the next three years, Sarah and Jill lived with us. It was sometimes difficult. It was also wonderful. They went to church with us. Sarah definitely struggled with our church family, and there were also times that our church really struggled with her. Sarah had a hard time with structure. She found a job, and I took care of Jill while she worked. Sarah's parents were not a good influence in her life and though they did have Jill in their home some for visits, they were not good for her. They took Sarah's struggles as a reflection on themselves and became defensive. They called me regularly and reminded me that they had four other "normal" children. They felt the problem was with Sarah and not them. This was the constant programming that Sarah had her entire life. She had certainly made plenty of mistakes in her young life, but was a good mother, very talented, and had a desire to do right. It was obvious that she had lived under an unhealthy label her entire life. It would take a lot of encouragement for her to see herself differently.

We had enrolled Leah in high school about the same time that Sarah and Jill came (we had been homeschooling her prior to this time). This was the first time since we were married that I did not have a child at home. As much as I did not want to see Leah go to public school, I was looking forward to some free time. Jill was more than I bargained for! My heart was to help young women, but I was not a child-type person. Except for the Bible Club years earlier and taking a turn teaching a Sunday school class or serving in the nursery, children were not my thing. Sarah and Jill were a package. I had to accept that, and recognize that since God was leading in this direction, He would also give me grace. I came to love Jill. She tagged along with me during my day. I made time each day to play with her and read to her. I thanked the Lord for allowing me to sow into her young life. The Lord stretched me and then gave me enjoyment in that place of surrender.

Sarah worked for a local florist. When she was doing well,

she was a wonderful employee and a great mom. When she struggled, every area of her life revealed the struggle. Sometimes she would slip back into old ways and get her hands on some drugs. These were difficult battles for us, and we had to learn to take hard stands. It seemed to come in waves. She would be fine for a long time and then without warning we would be revisiting these places again. What I did realize was that the periods between failures were getting longer a part. I tried to encourage her in that observation.

One day I realized she was back into drugs again. I asked her for them. She said if I was going to make her leave, she was going to keep them. I made her give them to me and flushed them. Then I told her to pack her and Jill's things. I would take her wherever she wanted to go, but they were leaving. She had been warned, so I had to do it. She told me where to drive them and I deposited them in front of a house in a very bad area of town. This was not a small thing, and I cried, broken-hearted, all the way home because we had come to love them both dearly. They were like family. I reeled in the pain and felt that our investment into their lives had been wasted.

God taught us during this time that our service was to Him. If the person receiving ministry responded and benefited, that was wonderful. If it appeared that all our efforts were not making a difference, we had been obedient and our service was to Him. He accepted the ministry as our love gift to Him, and that's what really mattered. Our efforts were not a waste. I often struggled trying to learn this lesson. If I poured myself into someone's life and they didn't respond well, I felt like such a failure. I tried to figure out what I did wrong. The responsibility would weigh on me. I had to learn that I could not produce results. I had to be obedient to whatever I was instructed to do, and know that sometimes my efforts would simply be mercy poured into someone's life. There was no guarantee that if I did my part, someone else would do theirs. Because God had brought such healing and restoration into my life, I wanted it for others. But, there were times that my piece of ministry was added to what someone else had already done. Or it could be that my piece was a preparation step to pave the way for someone else to minister down the road. I revisited this place often as God worked this truth into my life. I had a bit of understanding into Paul's words penned in Colossians 1:29: *...I work and struggle so hard, depending on Christ's mighty power that works within me.*

We are here to partner with God and if lives are changed, it's because people have responded to His work in their lives. It's God's ministry and they're God's results. I'm called to be faithful, obedient, and to honor Him. This is a great protection over us from the Lord. We don't carry the burden, nor do we take credit for what only He can do. It is more important to do things God's way and leave the results to Him. *The horse is made ready for the day of battle, but victory rests with the Lord* (Pr. 21:31, NIV).

The next day, after leaving Sarah and Jill, I came down with a bad virus and was sick for days. Sarah called me and asked if we could meet and talk. I was too sick to meet with her for nearly a week. God was at work in the timing of our meeting. By the time we could meet, she was repentant and asked for another chance. She and Jill came back home with me and we started again. This experience was good for both of us. She came to value our home, but also the progress she had made. I was placed in a position of not being able to take her back until God had done the work in her — and me — that needed to be done. Sometimes we have to rest in God's timing and give space for Holy Spirit God to prepare and work.

Sarah and Jill lived with us until Jill was six. Because Sarah had to deal with her own problems while caring for her daughter, it was wonderful for her to have someone to share that responsibility with her. Being a single parent is difficult under the best of circumstances. Sarah needed accountability, but most of all she needed a cheerleader. Everyone needs to be encouraged. Everyone needs to be told that they can make it, that their failure is not what defines them, and that God is for them. We can fall prey to the enemy when we fail. He tries to tell us that this sin that we are being tempted with is no big deal, or that this sin is not going to make that big of a difference if we give in to it. However, once we give in to it, he is quick to call us a total failure. He tries to pour on the guilt and label us by it. Some things must be battled through with help from another person. We need support and encouragement to keep on keeping on, especially when it's a place where we've fallen again and again. As I look back at my church's response to our plan to care for those released from prison, I clearly see that in the midst of it, God was accomplishing His purposes and plans. There is never a time or circumstance that He is not able to redeem and use for His purposes and our blessing. Many times the obstacles that we must plow through are used to strengthen and equip us, but are also to allow for God's perfect timing. There have been many times in the walk along this path with God that I've realized the delay in things happening was not with others as much as it was with me. God is patient and continues to work with us and to get us through these hard places.

I reminded myself of this truth in the months ahead. Our friend, Mr. Clyde, continued to struggle with our family's path, and also with the support and encouragement we were receiving from John and Joan. Since he and John were close and enjoyed fellowship together, he seemed to take it personally. The tension in the church family continued to grow to the point where we wondered if we should leave the church. As we prayed about it, God told us that He was preparing a new church family for us, but we needed to wait on His timing and provision. Our position as a family was to forgive those who couldn't understand what we had been called to do and to continue to serve and worship in this church until He told us to leave. Sam and I continued to volunteer, serve on committees, go to church each week, and actively look for ways to show our love and support to our brothers and sisters in Christ. Forgiveness is the hardest with people whom you love. Love gives people the power to hurt you. We were loved by this church family, and we loved them too. Our children had grown up in this church. This church family had ministered to us through Sam's seven back surgeries. They helped us pull together a beautiful wedding for Tara by helping to make bridesmaids' dresses, preparing food for the reception, and they had always shared freely with us. Though many struggled when we brought ladies from the prison to church with us, they did support the prison Bible study and our work there. I knew that Sarah and Jill had been a stretch at times for them, but they tried to offer support in spite of their inability to understand. We had beautiful relationships with these brothers and sisters in Christ. The friction caused from this situation was difficult. We felt like trouble makers and were viewed that way as well.

My heart was heavy as I watched Mr. Clyde grow increasingly fearful. I tried to rebuild our relationship and would walk over and chat, or wave. When we did talk, I would be careful not to bring up the prison class at all. He often changed the subject back to that discussion and tried to get me to see his perspective. The interaction became so difficult that I had to stay away. I realized that fear had become his prison. I understood that his fear about a prisoner living close to him was not personal against me, but a place from which only God could deliver him. I felt that he was crying out for help, but those cries were falling on deaf ears. We loved him and wanted him to have freedom from this unreasonable fear, but it seemed that as a church we were only enabling it to continue and to grow. In the family of God, we are too quick to cover over something for the sake of peace. Yet, this was not peace. Peace comes as we learn to progressively walk in truth. Being afraid to confront and address needs because we are worried about offending someone does not help anyone.

There were many times when we were tempted to give up and quit pursuing what God had put in our hearts. Friction and disagreements are difficult. But, we had lessons we needed to learn. In the midst of what seemed like the enemy having a heyday, God was at work. He could even use this as His training ground for us. We couldn't be responsible for what others needed to learn or what might have been handled poorly. We were too busy dealing with ourselves and what God was teaching us. We would not allow all of this to be wasted. We were going to glean all the good possible from this time. We didn't realize at the time how important these lessons were in order for us to stay on His path in the years to come. God was continuing to connect

His dots. He had us on His learning curve.

Mr. Clyde was repeatedly going to the leadership with concerns about our family and about John's relationship with us. One night I was called to another meeting. He was there when I arrived and so was John. The leaders were perplexed as to how to handle this. Mr. Clyde and his family were pillars of the church. They listened to him and then asked me questions. Every time I tried to speak, Mr. Clyde would interrupt. I couldn't believe that we were in this hard place. We'd had a beautiful friendship and had seen God work through many things as we prayed together. Mr. Clyde shocked all of us at the meeting when he accused me and John of having an adulterous relationship. The leadership knew there was no truth to it, but they had no idea how to handle him. Mr. Clyde was desperate to be heard and was trying anything possible to be make his point. The leadership was very unhappy with our family and ministry. I asked them what I was supposed to do. This was how God was leading our family. They had no response for me. I knew they were struggling, too. This was hard on everyone.

I returned home in tears, with frustration that I could hardly contain. Sam and I talked and prayed for a long time after I got home. I shared with him the accusations and my concerns on how all of this was escalating. We were crying out to the Lord for clarity. How did we get in this situation? We loved this church family. We loved Mr. Clyde. This could not be happening to us. There had to be a solution. Part of our frustration in this situation was the truth that our brother in Christ, Mr. Clyde, was struggling and needed help. There seemed to be no understanding that this was an opportunity to help someone who was dealing with a fear that Jesus could heal.

Another great concern that we had was how all this was affecting our children—especially Leah. I hated watching Leah struggle with our church family. We tried to keep it from being a topic of conversation at home. We were determined not to disrespect those God had placed in leadership over us. We had to continually speak the truth that God was at work, that we all had much to learn, and that God would bring resolution to this in His time and way.

Sometime later that evening, we saw car lights as a vehicle pulled into our driveway. It was John. He passed our house on his way home and saw we were still up. He was concerned for us and stopped to see if we needed anything. For a long time, the three of us talked and prayed together. We walked out to his car as he was leaving. Standing under the "talking tree," John spoke to Sam and me with a Spirit-filled challenge. God was speaking to us directly through him. We, he said, were being called by God down a path that would be a permanent change in our lives. He asked if we were prepared to say yes to the Lord in this place. We were both under great conviction that God had brought us to this crossroad. We accepted God's charge. Suddenly Holy Spirit God's presence was so very powerful under that tree that I could not stand up under the weight of His presence. John's car door was open and I slipped into the driver's seat and was limp in the presence of this Mighty God. There is no way to describe the magnitude of this God appointment. I had never experienced Holy Spirit God's presence in such a tangible and amazing way. On that night, in that private moment, we were anointed by Holy Spirit God for ministry, and experienced the touch of God. We knew life was getting ready to change.

These were hurtful times, but they were also important and growing times. It was definitely a bittersweet season. We could either side with the enemy and choose to label our precious brothers and sisters in Christ negatively, or we could side with the Lord. God was teaching us great truths, but also how to walk out those truths. Daily I declared aloud the countless blessings that I now enjoyed because of this beautiful church family. I would remind myself in the presence of the Lord how much I loved, respected, and was blessed by the influence of Mr. Clyde in my life and my family. My sweet Leah was one of hundreds of little children that had learned the love of Jesus from this amazing man of God. Mr. Clyde was not perfect, but neither was I. God doesn't require us to be perfect to be useful to Him. I would not throw away the good because of a rocky path! There was so much more to rejoice in than this one much shorter season of misunderstanding and hurt. When Satan served up the hurt, I replaced that thought with a good memory. This became a powerful weapon against the enemy. Remembering the good helped my emotions calm down, and it caused Satan to retreat. He doesn't want us to remember the good. My broken heart allowed me to see God's heart. It became an opportunity along my path to one day lead a ministry that focused on unity. This is truly beauty from ashes. I will spend eternity with these caring believers, and our amazing God will bring healing to all these hurts. We will enjoy God's redemption. They didn't handle everything the right way, but none of us do—especially me! As believers, we are all loved equally by God and these places of struggle do not define us. We are holy, loved children of the King of Glory.

***

John started a Bible study for couples at the church, open to anyone who wanted to attend. The study was from Henry Blackaby's *Experiencing God.* I had taught the series at the prison and the ladies had flourished under the teaching. We watched the class become a little church within the prison as they studied the principles taught in this study. It was a beautiful tool of God. I shared with John how much this study had been a blessing to me. He prayed over it and felt God would have him teach it at church. Many of us at the church formed a greater bond with each other as we also did this series together. It stimulated us to think deeper about outreach and leadership.

As the study continued, the leaders in the church no longer felt they could support it. They made the decision not to allow us to do it at the church building, so we had to meet in homes to complete the study. By the time the class was complete, some of the study attendees went to church leadership to ask them to consider making some changes within the church. Those requests were denied, and blame was cast on John as a divisive troublemaker. As a group, we prayed for our leaders and cried out to God to show us how we could make a difference in our church. We knew it wasn't God's plan for this study to cause problems. We needed to honor Him in this time. There was never any talk of leaving the church. Our hearts were set on honoring God in the church where He had called us.

One Sunday morning, as I was spending time with the Lord, He told me that this would be our last day at this church. Sam, Leah, and I prayed about this and also called Tara and Greg to ask them to pray. We were not sure what was going to happen, but as we drove to church that morning, we had heavy but expectant hearts. An announcement was made that morning that John was considered rebellious to the leadership authority and would no longer be considered part of our church. We were stunned and in shock. How could this be happening to our church family? Those of us who were excitedly learning through the study, and had developed deeper relationships as a result, were perplexed as to the next step. For our family, we knew what it meant. God had said to us over two years prior that He was preparing a new place for our family, and this very morning He had shown us that it was time to move on. We were sad that this was the process to that provision. It was not the heart of God for a new church to be started in this way. Anyone who is the parent of more than one child can understand the hurt that comes when children lash out at each other. I couldn't begin to imagine the pain this brought to our loving Father God to have His children behave with such unkindness toward each other. John had made a beautiful difference in this church. He had been used by God to help many of us grow in our relationship with the Lord. To label him as rebellious was far from the truth. He had been a servant of God to this church. He worked hard to try to bridge the gaps that were created when leadership refused to see the needs within the family of God. This was awful!

The next Sunday, many of those who had been meeting together to do the Bible study started a new church. It was painful to think that a resource as good as this study was used by the enemy for division. In reality, it hadn't. The study had been used by Holy Spirit God to stimulate a deeper understanding of church and family. Many things came together which brought this situation into place. The heartbreak over this crisis was indescribably painful, but a burden for displayed unity was being born in us. Just as He had done many times in the past, God reminded me that both He and Satan are at work using the same circumstances of life. When difficulties come, God wants to use those places to grow and to bless us. Our enemy tries to use those same places for evil. We get the amazing privilege of claiming them as Kingdom victories by how we respond and allow God to work in and through us.

Sam and I made some phone calls and wrote letters to the leadership and others at the church, thanking them for all they meant to our family, and telling them how much we loved and valued them. We tried to explain that we were following God's direction for our family and were not leaving angry or upset with anyone. The circumstances that brought things to this point made it difficult for folks to really understand and receive this as true. We understood that it was another place that we were misunderstood. I knew that even these attempts to speak truth and affirmation could not be valued by everyone, but we had to try.

A few days later I was grocery shopping and ran in to a good friend from our church. She and I had enjoyed fellowship together many times, and our family had often enjoyed dinner in her home. We served together on several committees and had never had a harsh word between us. As we chatted that day, she said to me, "God said to me that our church would be fine now that all the troublemakers were gone." It hurt my heart that she believed God would label His children as troublemakers. God calls His children "saints" or "beloved" or "righteous," but not "troublemakers." Part of the process of learning my identity in Christ was that God taught me to never label myself or another believer by poor behavior. Even with my children, I had learned to address the sin without allowing it to become their identity. I could address lying by saying something like: "in this family, we don't lie, or lying is not acceptable, or that is a lie," but never say "you are a liar."

I realized that God had us stay with this church family and

work on relationships for two years (after telling us He was preparing a new place for us) because He was doing a work in us. He was helping us understand how important it is to value the Family of God. Church hopping is a huge problem in the Body of Christ. We get upset with each other and instead of working through our differences and choosing love, we pack up our families and go somewhere else. Instead of using the hard places to grow, we go to a new place and soon become unhappy there, too. We act like spoiled children demanding our way, our comfort, our focus, and our agenda. We forget that being in a family means setting aside our own agenda, and together, seeking God's. We act like church is all about us instead of all about God. Family is a big deal to God. Working through this process and beginning to understand God's heart for family would become foundational to our future ministry at WLFJ. For now, our hearts ached and our emotions reeled as we tried to get our balance for the next step along God's path for us.

Chapter 7
Jesus is the Answer

The Lord says, 'I will guide you along the best pathway for your life. I will advise you and watch over you...'
Psalm 32:8, NLT

God took me to the end of Acts 2, where the church was unified and excited about what God was doing. Daily, Holy Spirit God added to the Body and needs were being met. In our new church we were experiencing this beautiful place. Most of those making up this new church had studied *Experiencing God* together. We hungered for God to show up among us and for there to be real and genuine fellowship. There was a deep place of love and acceptance in this new church family. We loved being together and looked for ways to make that happen. Worship was vital and real. Prayer meetings on Tuesday nights consisted of long periods of worship and strategic, anointed praying. We were filled with thanksgiving for all that God was doing among us. The prison class was embraced as a part of this church. Every Sunday, ladies came from the prison Bible class to join us for church. We had a potluck dinner each week so that we could feed these sisters in Christ before they went back. Needs in the Body were met quickly and quietly. John was the pastor of the church with several others joining him in leadership.

I was enjoying some time with the Lord early one morning, and He spoke to me from Isaiah 43:5-6: *Do not be afraid, for I am with you; I will bring your children from the east and gather you from the west. I will say to the north, Give them up! And to the south, Do not hold them back. Bring my sons from afar and my daughters from the ends of the earth.* He was going to bring Tara and Greg back to the east coast! I was so excited. I called Tara and told her that they were moving back to the east coast. I will never forget her response. She said, "Mom, does the U.S. Navy know that?" We chuckled together but knew God had spoken. We could not wait to see how God was going to do this. Greg was stationed on the USS Nimitz. A couple of weeks later, I got a call from Tara. The Navy was taking nuclear weapons off the Nimitz. The weapons were Greg's assignment, so he would be leaving the ship. They were sent back to the east coast for Greg's re-training, and then they were permanently stationed in Newport News, VA. Aaron was now a little over a year old and they were expecting Victoria's arrival in a few months. Again, God was reminding me that you will never go wrong when you surrender to God's plans and purposes. He loves to bless His children. Years later we would understand that God was working a plan together that we knew nothing about at the time. He was preparing us to be two of the three families that He would allow to steward His ministry called With Love From Jesus Ministries. Again, dots were connecting for a future time at WLFJ.

Living three hours apart was wonderful. When you never expect to see each other, a three-hour drive is nothing. I could drive up in one day and bring back a grandchild to spend a few days with us. When Victoria was born, and a few years later when Caroline joined their family, I would go and spend time with Tara. It was wonderful to live so close. Often the trips were quite interesting. One morning as I was driving to Newport News to get children, I noticed a car following closely on my bumper. The driver soon came up beside me and paced himself to my speed. As I glanced his way, he held up a huge sign on a piece of cardboard that read: rear passenger tire flat. That jolted me into attention. I had been blasting my praise music and singing along, enjoying the Lord, and hadn't noticed anything. I looked at my gasoline gauge and it was nearly on empty. I don't know how long I had been driving with that flat, but it was obviously a while.

On another trip, I was nearly there when I stopped for something to drink. When I got back in the car, it would not shift into third gear. I drove it the rest of the way, creeping along in second. The next day Greg followed me across town as we took it to someone recommended by his church. The mechanic looked at it and said the cost would be about $1,200, which was impossible because I didn't have it and the car wasn't worth it. Greg headed to the hospital to visit Tara and their new baby, and I began the slow process of getting back to their apartment in second gear. As I was going through town I passed a transmission shop. The Lord said to stop and talk to them about the car. I explained to them what had happened. The mechanic took a look at it, replaced a bolt, charged me twenty-five dollars, and I was on my way. The car never gave us any more transmission trouble.

Now that we were in this wonderful adventure with our new church, Tara and Greg came regularly for the weekend and worshipped with us. They loved being a part of this new work and watching all that God was doing. They were praying for us and were interested in all that was happening in the home ministry.

God did another unexpected thing. It was re-enlistment time for Greg. After eight years of being in the Navy, God spoke to Greg that he should not re-enlist. He was to get out of the Navy. This was the only life they had known as their own family. Greg had been in the Navy just a short time when he and Tara married. Their friends and their church in Virginia were very important to them, but God's Word to them was that they were to move back to Raleigh to help with the ministry Sam and I had in our home. None of us were sure what that would look like, but we knew God had spoken. Greg's Navy buddies gave him a hard time about leaving and often mocked him, asking what kind of a job he expected to get. Greg and Tara had not expected this change so the days ahead were busy as they tried to figure out the logistics of how to walk this out. The Lord was faithful to them. He provided Greg a job in Raleigh through a phone interview with a man that he had never met. The other fun thing that happened was the small house beside ours became available for rent and was reasonable. Our little church, which was just getting started, jumped in and helped us to paint and decorate in order to get Tara and Greg's first non-navy home ready for them. We were all excited and wondered what God was up to. Tara and Greg quickly found their own place in this new church. What fun it was for us to have Greg and Tara and their growing family as our neighbors. This unexpected and delightful surprise was more than we had ever hoped would happen. They were our neighbors and part of our church. God's ways are perfect.

While Sarah and Jill had lived with us, they'd loved going to our new church and were immediately pulled into the Body with much love and acceptance. Leah, who had really struggled during the last two years of our previous church situation, found a place of service and acceptance. The men's prison ministry was growing and we were often able to have one or two of the men from that class visit with us on Sundays as well. The maternity home that my friend Amy directed joined us regularly. Two other families were led by the Lord to take people into their homes to provide a place of care and discipleship. It was a time of rich blessing and peace. Our past experiences caused us to value this even more.

Earlier the Lord had said that He was going to move us to another house, but the time was not right. John and his business partner (who also attended our church) heard of a house that would soon be for sale. It was currently tied up in court litigations. A brother in Christ was the executor of the estate, which a family had been disputing over for some time, and the house was empty. We got permission to see it. It was within walking distance of our new church. We stepped into the house and it was love at first sight. The house had only three bedrooms but had two and half baths. The living room was huge with a big dining room and very nice kitchen. All the bedrooms were large. It had a sun porch, laundry room, and a two-car garage. On an acre of land, there was plenty of room to expand. The Lord confirmed to us that this was the place He had promised. John asked the executor to see if the courts would allow us to rent the house while it was in litigation. We secured a lease, and John's business rented the house for us. They would later purchase the house through their business.

Sarah got married, so she and Jill moved away. Leah graduated from high school and went on an all-summer mission trip. Sam and I, with the help of our amazing church, moved into our new home. We had lived in the farmhouse for fifteen years. The rent went up one time from $165 to $180 during those years. It was a wonderful place of blessing and had been used mightily by the Lord for our family and the greater Body of Christ. We were excited for this new adventure but left with the feeling of leaving an old friend behind. God had moved us to that farmhouse and it was what we could afford. We could never afford this new place, but God had covered even that. In all these years of ministry we had never had any financial support. We were just doing what God called us to do and never expected or thought about anyone helping us with the expenses. We were moving into a house that would soon be purchased by brothers in Christ who had a vision for what God had given us. This was more than anything we ever expected.

Before Leah came home from her summer mission trip, Donna and her little daughter, Ellie, moved in with us. Donna was another prisoner but not from the prison. We came to know Donna through her sister who lived with another member of our church. Donna and Ellie lived with Donna's mother. Donna had many health needs and suffered greatly from migraine headaches. She had severe scoliosis and was in pain all the time. She spent most of her time in bed, couldn't eat, and little Ellie did whatever she pleased. At two she was a handful! Donna's mother was a big part of the problem, she treated Donna badly, and seemed indifferent to her daily needs.

With the restrictions gone from us, Sam and I were excited

about the potential of helping someone from the prison class, but the Lord very specifically directed us to Donna. We knew this was His plan. It was a challenging season with Donna and Ellie. Ellie had no discipline and was much like a little wild, untamed adventurer. She had no fear and no regard for structure or correction. The first day Donna was with us, I spent the entire day in the emergency room with her getting medication for pain. We started praying daily over her body. We dealt with all the strongholds from her past that were holding her captive. We put discipline and structure in place for Ellie. Donna was so thin that she looked like she would break in half. Having spent my entire life struggling with my own weight, I could not identify with Donna's lack of desire to eat. I cried out to the Lord for wisdom and understanding. He gave us a plan. Every couple of hours I would take Donna a few crackers or a small piece of fruit. At first she didn't want it, but I told her she had to at least try to eat a few bites each time. We did this routine for a couple of weeks and the food introduced to her system began to produce a little bit of an appetite in her. Soon she was eating three small meals every day and keeping them down. The more she ate, the more her body desired food. Gradually she began to gain weight. There have been many times over the years that I have recommended this to believers who were struggling with no appetite for things of the Lord. I encourage them to take ten minutes several times each day to read a verse of scripture or seek God in prayer asking Him to use this to stimulate an appetite for Him. When I find myself waning in my own desire for things of the Lord, this is a quick way to get refocused and rekindled in my own walk with Jesus. A verse of scripture written on a slip of paper and tucked in my pocket would often become a way to savor the Word as I ran across it all during the day.

Donna and I spent many hours together working through forgiveness issues. She had many! As she dealt with forgiveness, her headaches began to go away. She could sit in the yard and let Ellie play outside. I would give her a handful of M&Ms or a few miniature marshmallows. As Ellie was playing, Donna would call her. When she came, Donna would give her a small treat. We did this day after day until Ellie developed an ear to hear Donna call and also learned to obey. Within a year, Donna was able to do housework, her own laundry, and grew in her relationship with the Lord. She enjoyed church. Our church family offered help in caring for Ellie and transporting Donna to her appointments.

For Donna it was a slow but steady pace of learning to walk with the Lord and being brave enough to take those needed growth steps. By her second year with us, she was able to get a job at a daycare center near our house. She worked and took Ellie with her. It was a great situation. Her eyesight had been poor, but had improved so she could learn to drive. She also saved up money for a car. In three years she went from being bedridden much of the time to being self-sufficient and capable of working, driving, and parenting Ellie.

Leah was working two jobs and moved out on her own to live nearby. Sam had been injured years earlier on his job and was not able to work. He was on disability and dealing with pain each day. He was home and available to help transport ladies to work, or appointments, or help with the many activities of our busy home. The flood gates opened as ladies from the prison began to travel through our home and church at a steady pace. We were watching God work in ways that He had promised He would work. Captives were set free. We learned how to minister to people in difficult circumstances. Every new person was a learning experience. God was growing them and us.

Ladies in the prison Bible study began to realize that some were moving in with our family when they left prison. Many asked if they could live with us upon release. I knew we would one day need to cross this bridge. God gave me His answer for them. I always said that I'd love to have them live with me. However, we would need to first ask God His perfect plan for them. If His plan was for them to stay with us for a while, He'd make it known to them and to me. If He did not direct us in that way, we would together seek God's perfect plan for them. This always satisfied and always affirmed. Everyone needs to know that God has a plan for them and it is a plan of blessing, hope, and a great future. Everyone is different. Many would come through our home, but many more would not. Sometimes ladies needed to break all ties and connections to the prison when they moved on to a new life. We totally understood that.

Rebecca was one of those sweet ladies who, once she was released, moved on not to be heard from again for a long time. Seventeen years after she was released, however, she did make contact with me. What a blessing to hear from her again. I am always interested in knowing how God is at work in someone's life. Rebecca came to prison as a young, single mom of a two-year old. Her incarceration was short term as her offense was minor. However, even a couple of years can be a long time when you have a small child.

We watched Rebecca grow and absorb the teaching during the prison Bible study. More importantly, she learned to put it into practice. When she returned home, she attended one church for a while but realized she was struggling to maintain a consistent walk with the Lord. She pulled out her old Bible study notes from the prison Bible study and began to focus on her identity in Christ. Rebecca began to walk those truths again. She looked for the right church for her that would help her stay focused. She found a wonderful church that taught with a great emphasis on her identity in Christ, and also encouraged walking in the power of the Holy Spirit. She had a long drive each week to go to church but felt it was well worth the investment for her and her daughter. Rebecca grew in her walk with the Lord and eventually married a godly man. She began to teach freedom and identity in Christ to the youth in her church and saw many set free. God gave her and her husband a ministry with couples in their church.

God was using her past for good. Her incarcerated time was being redeemed for the Kingdom. He even gave her a young woman in prison that called her twice each week for prayer support and discipleship. One day she was cleaning out papers from an old Bible and found a letter I had written to her years earlier when her daughter was little. At that time, she was trying to help her daughter work through their separation. She re-read the letter, and realized that the young woman she was discipling in prison needed this same advice. That woman had a four-year old son. Rebecca shared the truths from a seventeen-year-old letter with this young woman. God's truth never grows old. The letter was still in its original envelope so she used that address to reach out to me. We were excited to be able to talk and catch up after all those years.

God had burdened Sam and me for these precious ladies. He had made a way for us to minister to them. We were blessed and enjoying God's provision for this beautiful ministry.

Helen came to know the Lord in the prison class. She was funny and always a delight to be around. She also struggled greatly. She was from a huge family as her dad had been in multiple relationships and there were many children. Their family was also dysfunctional. As release came near for Helen, she asked if she could live with us. As a family, we prayed and God directed us to invite her to come. She was excited. She was serving her entire sentence so she would not be on parole. The plan was that she would call me from the prison once she had been processed and was ready to leave, and I would come for her. If you are not paroled, you simply walk away. The prison gives you a few dollars, you leave and are on your own. We knew the day that she was likely to be released and waited all day for her phone call. It never came. It didn't happen the next day or the next. We realized that she had made another choice. The following Wednesday night, when I went for Bible study, the other ladies told me that someone from her home had picked her up. We were so sad. We continued to pray for her and asked God to protect her and have her call us. She had our phone number, but we had no phone number for her.

One Sunday morning while worshipping the Lord with our wonderful church, God spoke to me. He said, *"The good shepherd leaves the ninety-nine to look for the one that is lost."* I knew immediately that He was speaking to me about Helen. Sam and I discussed it that afternoon. We needed to make arrangements for someone to help with Donna and Ellie, but first thing Tuesday morning we headed out to look for Helen. Her family lived about an hour and a half from us. We had a street address but nothing else and there was no GPS at that time. When we arrived in her hometown, we stopped to get a bite to eat and a mailman happened to be there having his lunch. We asked him if he knew the address and he was able to give us directions. We arrived and were told that Helen was visiting someone a couple houses down the street. One of her younger sisters ran to get her. When Helen saw us, she fell into my arms crying. She was very un-kept in her appearance and obviously had been on drugs. We talked and prayed with her. She decided to come home with us. She climbed into the backseat of our car with no possessions. These few weeks since leaving prison had been hard for her.

She loved our church and loved our family. We loved her, too. She enjoyed the Word and fellowship with the Body. She struggled but kept trying. She lived with us for several months, got back on her feet, found a job, and seemed (in her eyes) ready to be on her own. A few months later, she was back in prison and attending Wednesday night Bible study again. After she was released this time, she was stronger. She did much better. She didn't live with us again, but she visited regularly. It wouldn't be unusual for me to answer the phone and it be Helen. We would sometimes see an unknown car pull in the driveway, and Helen would get out. She eventually became more stable in her walk with the Lord and got married.

We had to face the fact that sometimes we were called to sow into someone's life for a few days, months, or even years. We had no control over how someone would steward the time invested in them. That was between them and God. Our position was to surrender them to Him and His work in their lives and know that it was our love gift to the Lord as we gave our time and resources to someone. God says that whatever we do for a brother or sister in the family of God, we have done for Him. He reminds us that to give to the poor is to give to Him. It was His ministry and He could use whomever He pleased. It was a blessing to know that sometimes He was pleased to use us. God is everybody's answer. He will not let someone or something else become their answer. We get the privilege often of being a part of how He's at work in someone's life, but only a part. These would be important connecting dots for us later as we served at WLFJ. God would never let us be someone's answer. He would use us at times, but He is the real answer that never fails.

* * *

One morning, after we had moved to our new home, someone knocked on Tara's door. She answered it to find a bulldozer parked in her driveway. The man at the door was shocked that someone was living in the house. The house had been sold and was being demolished to build an office building there. Their landlord had given them no warning. They were not even aware that the house was for sale. The man with the bulldozer said he would come back in a week and give them time to move out. We were overwhelmed and cried out to the Lord for direction for them. The temporary solution was that they would move in with us. Our house was already very full. Donna and Ellie lived with us at the time, and this was before Helen had moved out. We moved Tara and Greg into the sunroom, camped the kids on the floor, and stored their things in the garage as we sought God's plan for their next step. Helen soon moved, but her room was not empty for long.

My mother had been sick for some time. She was in the hospital and wanted to go home, but it was impossible for Dad, whose health was also failing, to meet her needs. My brother lived in Florida and my sister lived in a small mobile home. Mother didn't want to come to our house because, to say the least, we were quite odd! Her doctor gave her the choice of either going to a nursing home or moving in with us. She moved in and lived with us for a few weeks before her death.

This was a great privilege for me and for our family. Both of my parents came from very large families. My dad's family had fifteen children and mom's had thirteen. I'm sure her memories of such a busy household were not always good. There were many problems and needs in her family growing up. At times, she must have had a hard time separating these feelings from our busy household. Mom had often struggled with our unusual way of life. During these weeks we had many good chats. I loved seeing her peacefulness. In the beginning it was difficult for her to allow us to serve her, but as the days went by, she relaxed and enjoyed our time together. Every day Dad would come and spend time with her. Tara's children were a delight to Mother. We were careful to keep her room quiet but they were supervised and allowed to visit her every day. One day she said to me, "Linda, this is a very pleasant place." That was a huge statement for her to make. God was pouring His peace into our home. The activity in it was all from Him and all was good. While Mother was living with us, something devastating happened.

Chapter 8
Past Faithfulness Lights the Path for Today's Steps

He holds victory in store for the upright, he is a shield to those whose walk is blameless, for he guards the course of the just and protects the way of his faithful ones. Then you will understand what is right and just and fair—every good path.
Proverbs 2: 7-9, NIV

Our world was about to be rocked, but the One who holds the world in His hands was in charge. One of my closest friends and a partner with Joan and me in the prison Bible study was obviously going through a difficult time. I could tell by our conversations that something was not right. When she and her husband came to prayer meetings, it was apparent that they were struggling in their relationship. At the same time, John seemed to also be going through a difficult time and had lost his zeal for the church. He seemed to suddenly be dealing with burnout. It became common knowledge to everyone within just a couple of weeks that sin had invaded our beautiful and growing church.

We were heartsick. We had warred together through many difficult times, and this was totally unexpected. As a church we tried to minister to those caught in this trap, but without success.

When God has used someone in your life or ministry in the incredible way that God had used John, it's easy to forget that they are human, too. We are sometimes guilty of expecting them to walk to a higher standard than others or not to be vulnerable to temptation in the same ways. It's easy to forget to come beside them with support and prayer. The greater someone is used by the Lord, the greater the enemy wants to wipe out their effectiveness. I suspect that our church expected John to be above this place of temptation and therefore neglected to watch over him. Looking back, there were signs that I should have recognized. A good friend should have asked more questions and been more watchful. His love for the Lord was great, yet temptation was also great. I know that this was not as sudden as it seemed. This did not happen overnight. It was a process of one thought that wasn't captured becoming an action, and then another action, only appearing to be sudden. It's easy to arrive at a place that you never intended to go. It could have been prevented, especially with help.

It reminds me of David when he was king. The scriptures reveal to us that he was a man after God's heart. No one expected him to take such a hard fall. Wouldn't his love for God outweigh these deep temptations? There were symptoms that showed he was possibly struggling or not handling life as normal. For example, not going to war when that was his typical duty at that time of year. He became vulnerable and showed his humanity in a shocking way. David's downward spiral is painful to read. David fell, and he hurt many people in the process. The Word doesn't hold back from revealing David's failure because God wants us to profit from it. Our God wants us to be warned, of course, but He also wants us to understand that nothing can separate us from His love. A fall doesn't change God's love or His ability to continue to use someone. It does sometimes make a difference in how that person will be used in the future, or may require that person to be set aside for a while. Jesus paid it all.

It's not about punishment. It's about redeeming! Forgiveness is instant, but recovery takes time. Nothing is wasted with God.

Very quickly our church split as it reeled from the pain. The next days were horrible. Members left as they reacted to this hard and unexpected situation. We couldn't blame our brothers and sisters in Christ who left. We all wanted to run somewhere and hide. This felt like too much to bear. Four years earlier we started this great adventure as a new church and now an unpredicted and painful event was hitting us extremely hard. Over the next few months, the church progressively lost members each week. We called special meetings and tried to work through the growing issues and misunderstandings. Each attempt seemed to only make things worse. There was one final split which left only a few members and the three couples in leadership. We went to those who left to try to minister to them. We were also dealing with our own pain. Most whom we talked to wanted to move on and felt the church could not recover. God clearly directed those of us that were left to stay together. It was not our place to judge anyone who left; everyone needed to decide what was best for their own family and how God was leading them. Our fragmented church needed ministry, but there seemed to be no one to call for help. Could God possibly be calling us to throw away four amazing years and move on? There was someone to help. His name is Jesus. He had not abandoned us!

Kevin was the brother in Christ who had taken over the role of pastor after John left. Kevin and his wife, Shelly, were one of the three couples left after the church split, along with Tara, Greg, Sam, and me. The church could no longer support Kevin. His family went through a rough time. He tried to minister to the many that were hurting, but nothing seemed to work. In reality, we were all in pain and struggling to the point that no one really knew what to do. Within a few months, Kevin's family lost their home, which left them in great need. Our household felt that we had been hit from every direction. Tara and Greg's sudden loss of their house, my mom's sickness and death, and now the loss of our church family had left us stunned.

We felt forsaken by our church family at a time when we

longed for their support and help. My mom's sickness was hard for our family and the crowdedness of our home brought many difficulties. We longed for our church family to jump in to help with meals or other support during this time, but it was not there. Many good things were happening in the deepening of my relationship with my parents. It would have been wonderful to have believers to share these things with us. We felt alone and completely isolated. We appreciated the love and support of my brother, Larry, during these days. He was states away, but he called almost daily and sent money for us to grab take-out meals for our busy household. My sister was full of pain and dysfunction in her own life. She wanted to help and tried several times to come and stay with mom so I could nap or run errands. Her help was appreciated and challenging at the same time. She was critical of our care for Mother and pointed out all the ways she wanted it done differently. These were important days for me to forgive her and love her and not allow myself to be stuck in an emotional trap. I understood that she was dealing with her own deep emotions and sense of helplessness. She was doing the best she could, and I loved her, and appreciated the hard place she was in at the same time. I looked for every opportunity to minister to her, but she couldn't receive it. To say the least, life was feeling out of control.

Shortly after my mother died, Kevin's family moved in with us. They were a family with three children of their own and a foster child. They didn't have family in our area and now this difficult place left them without their basic needs being met. We could not desert them. We knew God would meet their need. It also seemed that we were the instrument God had chosen to use. With ladies from the prison, Greg and Tara's family, and now adding Kevin's family, there were seventeen of us living in a three-bedroom house. What in the world was happening? What was God up to? What was our next step? It all seemed bizarre, unreal, and a nightmare!

God had us firmly by the hand. He did not allow us to sink. The waves of life were huge, but all was fine! We had some experience under us that gave us a foundation that was part of His tool of blessing now. Nothing is wasted with God. He sustains and blesses us through hard times, and He then goes back to those old storehouses to pull from them and to continue to bless us.

Many years before, when we walked away from a lucrative business where we enjoyed a beautiful house and new cars, God put us on a path of learning and knowing Him and His ways which continues today. We left that world to experience more peace, joy, and satisfaction in life than we could have ever thought possible. There are plenty of people with great paying jobs, living in nice houses, and driving new cars that also experience this relationship. For us, the path would be different because God had a plan for us that He was unfolding. We had a lot to learn and to unlearn. God was training us for a future day when at WLFJ we would minister daily to families going through crazy and unusual situations that needed the same hope that God was infusing into us. We would meet many multi-family households that were trying to survive in a difficult world and needed encouragement.

Yes, with the split of the church, our house filled to overflowing with people, and the source of the provision for our current house was no longer in fellowship with us. We were headed down a bumpy path, but God had prepared us for this time with years of past faithfulness. We were thankful for all God had already taught us, but somehow this all seemed different. Every place of trial or growth seemed different, yet the lessons learned of our God's amazing faithfulness and sustenance are the same!

Another thing that happened about the same time was that the business partners called a meeting with Sam, Greg, Tara, and me to talk about the house situation. Their business had made a set of rules for how the ministry home should run, but had never shared those rules with us. One of the rules was that family members could not live in the house. They realized they had never given us a copy and regretted it, but still didn't feel that they should allow us to continue our current living situation. The Lord was gracious to us to help us understand that this was not about our family or even the home ministry. It was more fallout from the church split. These business partners who had once been part of our church family no longer had a heart for what God had called us to do. In fairness to them, we had to admit to ourselves that our family dynamics were changing, too. We were headed down an unexpected road that we had not seen in the past. This change must have seemed odd to them. The enemy had stirred up quite a mess, but God is a great redeemer and wastes nothing when it is given to Him. God's plan cannot be stopped!

We found God continually reminding us of an important lesson. When people disappoint or hurt us, it is easy to want to scrap the entire relationship, including the past good. God warned us not to go down that path. These precious brothers in Christ had been huge blessings to us. The current problems could not erase the Kingdom deposits they had made in our lives! I cannot imagine, or want to know, the number of people I have hurt and let down along my path. There was nothing intentional here. If I want forgiveness, I have to also be gracious and generous in my forgiveness to others. The very best example of this for me is that Holy Spirit God does not give up on me and throw me out when I let Him down or dishonor Him in our relationship. He loves me unconditionally, forgives me, and continues to want a relationship with me. In the Body of Christ, we all need each other. We cannot afford to write each other off when things don't go well.

An interesting and seemingly odd thing had happened in the midst of the church situation. A local grocery store told Kevin, our new pastor, that they were throwing away hundreds of dollars of food daily and asked if our church would be interested in having this food to give to needy families in the community. We began to pick up the food and quickly realized that the grocery store wanted it picked up six days each week. All of the people left in the church were involved in ministry and had busy lives, but we understood that this was an opportunity from the Lord. We knew we should at least begin to walk it out and see what happened. Our lives appeared to be full of puzzle pieces that were floating around and didn't seem to connect. God was getting ready to connect them for us. Looking back, it was an exciting time of watching God at work. At the time, it was grueling days of training by our King and Master.

Chapter 9
Seek His Kingdom First

For I am about to do something new. See, I have already begun! Do
you not see it? I will make a pathway through the wilderness. I will
create rivers in the dry wasteland.
Isaiah 43:19, NLT

When it seems that the bottom has fallen out of life, the goal of
our enemy's attack is to try to get us to figure out what we have
done wrong. If there is conviction of sin, we definitely need to
deal with it. Of course we want to draw near to God, listen to
hear His voice, and learn whatever we can through this time.
However, often the greatest step of faith we can take is simply
doing the last thing He told us to do, keeping an open heart and
mind to any new direction.

In the weeks since Tara and Greg's family had moved in
with us, we heard God speak in a way we were not expecting.
He was calling their family to share the ministry with us and for
us to live together. Apparently, our living arrangement was not

going to be a temporary situation. God gave us clarity that Greg's call out of the Navy and their relocation to Raleigh was Him preparing us for this time. We were faced with many upcoming changes and had no idea how to walk them out. After the meeting with the business team, we were told that we could either buy the house or move. Both options were impossible for us as we had a house full of people and little income. Sam's disability from a work related incident—which led to seven back surgeries—meant that he could no longer work. He was getting a small disability check each month. A family member of one of the partners came to us and said, "Well, I guess the free ride is over."

The sadness of how the enemy had gotten a foothold in this was unreal to us. These men had approached us and we had been ministering together to bless and encourage hurting people. We had served in this capacity for many years even before they came along. The house being covered by these business partners had been a perfect solution for us, causing our money to stretch, and also giving Sam the time he needed to help with the ministry. Greg was working in an entry-level position which provided them what they needed as a family, but not enough provision for purchasing a house. Kevin's family living with us was never intended to be permanent. This was a time for us to come alongside a family who had been knocked down by the very church they were trying to serve. They needed some time to regroup and receive support and ministry. Our direction from the Lord was to minister to them and encourage them, not judge their decisions as they walked out this difficult road. There would be many times in the years coming up that WLFJ would not only serve those in our community with need, but would also come alongside someone in ministry that needed help or encouragement. We were continuing down a path of God's design and blessing. If it hadn't been such an intense time, it really would have been almost comical! We were certainly in the fast lane of God's training.

From late May until early September of 2001, our household was unusually busy. Donna had married and she and her daughter were no longer with us. Our three bedrooms were filled with Sam and me in one, Tara and Greg in one, and their children in the third. We invited Kevin and Shelly to move into the sunroom. We made beds for their children on mattresses in the living room. During these struggling days, Kevin often said, "I never thought we'd be homeless." We reminded them that they were "houseless." Their family, their true home, was very much intact.

God dropped another puzzle piece into our laps. This piece came from the prison. A lady in the prison class had two children that were in an abusive situation in Montana. They had not seen their mom in a long time. A friend serving with me at the prison purchased plane tickets for the children to come and visit their mom. The plan was that they would stay with us for a couple of weeks. These plans were in place before Kevin's family lost their house. Once the children arrived, it became evident that they did not need to go back. The mom, who had a long-term sentence, had legal custody of the children and wanted to give us custody until she was released from prison. After much prayer, we had peace about it and agreed to take them. She understood the craziness of our household, but we all knew this was God at work. We made the living room into a girls' dorm and the dining room into a boys' dorm. At night we lined mattresses on the floor and bedded children down. The next morning, we stacked the mattresses against the wall in the garage and ran the household as efficiently as possible. In the evening, church-type tables were lined up end to end in the large living room so we could share a family meal together. In those days, it was important to minister to everyone's needs. The chaos and busyness demanded that we have structure with time to listen and care for every family member. One night during these months, a local Outback Restaurant treated the six adults in our household to a night out. God cared about even this!

The food ministry from the grocery store was time consuming as well. Our household developed a daily routine. One of the six adults went first thing each morning to pick up the food. It was brought back to our garage and sorted. We fed those in ministry and then bagged up all the rest and headed out into the community to give away the abundance. God directed us not to freeze or save food. We had to use and give away the food daily, as the next day there would be more. On your day to pick up food, it was also your responsibility to give it all away. Each of us had a different place that we would go when it was our turn. We divided up the workload at home as well. Some of us would care for children, some would do laundry and housework, and others would take care of the food ministry. Tara and I continued to go to the prison to minister. Kevin and Shelly had a membership to the YMCA, so on their day to care for children, they loaded up all the kids and took them for a swim. After swimming everybody got their showers and shampooed their hair at the facility as well. This took a load off our household to get everyone through bath time. The Lord reminded me again, as He often had in the past, that this storm would pass. Once it was gone, I would have been very unhappy with myself had I been fearful and doubtful instead of walking in trust. During this time, we were praying for God to reveal to us the next step. Daily, I would declare to God, "Father, to the best of our ability we are seeking you and your Kingdom and walking with integrity before you. If there is something we need to change, please show us. We are expectant that you will take care of us and give us your wisdom."

My journals during these days contained lists of needs such as utilities bills, gas for vehicles, clothing needs, car insurance, laundry detergent, stamps, haircuts, anointed time, wisdom to give to a lady I was counseling, provision to pay a doctor's bill, a date night out for me and Sam, and many more things. Beside each need I wrote "PTL" when it was provided. Our amazing God cared about all these things and more. He was, and continues to be, faithful!

This very declaration that God had us walk became the words of encouragement we gave to the community that soon came to WLFJ. We spoke with confidence that God had a plan of blessing for them in the midst of their place of need. Many in our community come looking for answers. They seem stuck in a place and don't know how to get out. We understand! However, God had given us a plan, and we could count on it to work. The secret to moving from this place of need to a place of advancement is simple. Seeking the Lord above everything else, honoring Him daily, and listening to Him with a heart ready to obey always promises blessing. It's the principle of God's Word. It works!

The Lord's instruction to us concerning the food ministry was that it was not about re-building our church. It was about the bigger Body of Christ. As we went out into the community each day, we said, "We are part of a food ministry and have extra food today. Could you, or someone you know, use a bag of groceries?" We never had anyone turn down the food. As we gave the food away we said, "Please receive this 'with love from Jesus'." We offered to pray with people. Some people received Christ. When someone came to know the Lord, we helped them find a church in their neighborhood to disciple and encourage them. By early September, Kevin's family was able to move into their own place, the two foster children staying with us moved into the sunroom, and life continued. With their new residence, Kevin and Shelly turned their basement into another sorting and staging place for the food ministry. We tried to get other churches to help us as we quickly realized this was too big for one very small church. God had called it to be about the greater Body of Christ, but because it was branded as part of our church ministry, it was difficult to get other churches to join us.

During the months that Kevin's family lived with us, we filed the paperwork to become a 501c3 so we could separate the ministry from the church and begin to establish it as an independent local nonprofit. We spent many evenings discussing this process together and making the decisions as Kevin filled out the application. One of those discussions was about the name of the ministry, which was required to apply for nonprofit status. The only thing that kept coming to our minds was what we said to people when we were delivering the food, "Please receive this with love from Jesus." The name of the ministry became With Love From Jesus Ministries. In October of 2001, eighteen months after beginning in two garages, WLFJ became a nonprofit. Kevin and Shelly took the role as co-directors for the next three years and we continued to work from our two homes. Then, another church joined us and a third home was established as a food location. We were now a nonprofit, but in reality, our daily activities had not changed. Everyone jumped in to do whatever was needed.

One of our first WLFJ stories was that of Candy, a single mom with two teenage daughters. Wednesday was one of my days to pick up the food. On this day, I had given away most of the food but still had a few bags left. Each Wednesday I traveled the same path in the evening as I headed to the prison to teach the Bible study. There were several people along that path that would be watching for me and would be blessed to receive food. On this particular day, after serving my regulars, I had three or four bags of groceries left to give away. It was a hot August evening and I knew, by the time I left the prison, the food would be spoiled. I began to pray that the Lord would show me who really needed these last bags of food. I was only two blocks from the prison and no one was on the street. This was odd because inner city Raleigh streets were usually filled with people, but the heat was oppressive, driving folks to seek shelter and a fan. A city bus was coming toward me on the opposite side of the street and made a stop. A lady got off the bus and crossed in front of me to the other side. She had to be the one! When I rolled down my window, she looked nervously at me. I told her I was part of a food ministry and had some left, and wondered if she could use it, or knew someone who could. She threw her arms up in the air and screamed, "Praise the Lord." It was Candy's first day on a new job. Someone had given her bus tickets so she could get to work and back. Her teenagers were at home waiting for her to return. There was no food at home. As she was riding the bus, she looked out the window and prayed that God would show her how to come up with dinner for her family when she got home. Candy climbed into my car and I gave her a ride to her apartment just a few blocks away. Candy became one of my regular stops on Wednesday nights as I headed to the prison.

After Kevin and Shelly's family moved into their own place, our life developed into a new routine. I was thankful that God had called Tara and Greg to join the home ministry and for us to all live together. The prison ministry was demanding and wonderful. Teaching the class each week, heading up a team, planning outings for the ladies, and working with the administration of the prison was time consuming for me. WLFJ was growing daily, and the demands connected with it were also great. We found ourselves with two foster children who had abundant needs. Even though they were now enrolled in school, they were behind. This was in addition to the challenges of being biracial, having a mom in prison, and a dad upset by his sudden loss of control over them. They had a lot to deal with—and so did we. We had no idea how long they would actually need to stay with us. We were committed to take it one day at the time. Tara spent many days running back and forth to their schools trying to get extra assistance for them, settling transition issues, and constantly being their advocate. She was amazingly anointed for this time. They had learned to cope with life in some unhealthy ways and living in a Christian home was a huge change for them, as well as a challenge and place of new growth for us. There were also some challenges for Greg and Tara's children as these new children were added to our busy household. They were already transitioning to all of us living together. Each day was full of adjustments and we were surprised by how well the days went. Tara was homeschooling her children at the time. It gave her one-on-one time with them before our new family members returned from school and needed extra help with their studies. The foster children's mom wanted them in public school because it would make life easier for them later when she was released to be a single, working mother. We could easily see God's wisdom in giving us four adults to shoulder this intense time.

We tried to find a balance between being an authority in the daily lives of these children, and not taking any authority away from their mom. They visited the prison with me each Wednesday night so they could spend time with their mom doing homework and getting to know each other a little better. We petitioned the prison for home visits for their mom. At first, she was allowed to come for a 5-hour visit. Soon she was able to come once or twice a month for an overnight stay. They needed a lot of help in re-establishing their relationship with each other and developing one with us. As the garage phase of WLFJ continued, they jumped in and helped with making up bags of food like everyone else in our household. We have fun pictures of children and food loaded up in vehicles as God allowed us to storm the gates of hell using bags of food as our entrance. Increasing numbers of people came to know the Lord as the teams began to invade more areas of our community. Our foster children loved being part of this outreach and both came to know Jesus during the time they lived with us.

Eighteen months into this unplanned adventure, I received a call from the parole board asking if we were willing to take the children's mom to live with us if she was paroled. Life was full and busy for us now as WLFJ was in its first real building and we were trying to figure out how to juggle a building across town instead of serving the community from our garage. Adding their mom was a new dynamic. We realized that God had used our constant presence at the prison, along with the fact that we had her children locally in our home, to give the children's mom favor with the parole board. We had no idea when the children came to live with us that this would be the case, but we rejoiced in seeing their family restored before the children were grown and no longer under her care. The walls of this amazing house continued to stretch as we added the children's mom to our full and busy household.

There were many times over the years that we witnessed the walls of our house stretch. Such was the case on a Wednesday night as I prepared to go to the prison to teach the Bible Study. One of the ladies in the class had already called with the concern that I might not come because a big storm was brewing. Then I received a phone call from the Superintendent advising me that one of our classmates was being released. When the release date arrives, there is no negotiating to stay longer regardless of the situation. Samantha had a place to go, but Hurricane Bonnie was currently bearing down on our coast, so buses were cancelled leaving her no way to get to her home located on the east coast. She needed a place to stay for a day or two until bus transportation was restored. Our household was full, but we welcomed Samantha to sleep on the couch. In the meantime, Leah came home and brought a friend with her who lived in a mobile home and needed a safe place to stay for the night. Before I could get out the door to the prison, James, a homeless man to whom our church had been ministering, called to say he had no place to go in the storm and all the shelters were full. Sam stepped in to minister to James so I could get to the prison. He gave James blankets and allowed him to bed down in our enclosed garage until the storm passed. This house has been a blessing to many. Soon thereafter, Leah gave us a doorknocker for the front door as a gift. It read, "I was a stranger and you welcomed me in." The Lord constantly reminds us that we were all strangers and He welcomed us into His family. This was a lovely gift from the Lord to allow us to continue to live in this house and minister in His name to many in our community.

The house crisis was a constant situation for us. The business team was pushing us to buy or get out, and now said we needed to pay rent until we made a decision. We pursued loan applications, which seemed futile with our small incomes. We cried out to the Lord for wisdom. God gave us peace that we should not pay the rent demands. We had no lease agreement because we had moved into the house with the understanding that this was a ministry partnership. We were still doing the same ministry we had agreed to do in the beginning. The entire time we were in the house, we always had at least one or more people with needs living with us. Even with our full household, we never failed to keep our end of the agreement. Before the Lord, we were at peace that we were fulfilling our part of the commitment. There were no funds for us to pay the rent, but we covered all the utilities and maintained the household as previously agreed upon. Every day we continued to declare before the Lord, and each other, our total dependence on Him. Each day we claimed the promise from His Word that if we would seek Him first, He would take care of our needs. The Lord gave us favor with a mortgage company, and unbelievably, we received a loan approval.

As we neared the closing date for the house, we felt anxious about what we were doing. We were taking on a mortgage payment with little income. Many people were living with us and depending on us. Portions from the Word continually came to my mind. In Joshua chapter one, Joshua was instructed to *not be afraid or discouraged*. He had the choice. He could either be discouraged or the opposite—encouraged! God instructed him to stay saturated in the Word of God, mediate on it, and obey it. From Lamentations 3:20b-26, I was reminded of a portion that God had given me many times in the past: *...my soul is downcast within. Yet this I call to mind and therefore I have hope: Because of the Lord's great love we are not consumed, for his compassions never fail. They are new every morning; great is your faithfulness. I SAY TO MYSELF* (emphasis mine), *'The Lord is my portion; therefore I will wait for him.' The Lord is good to those whose hope is in him, to the one who seeks him; it is good to wait quietly for the salvation of the Lord.*

God also took me to 1 Samuel 30. David and his men returned to their camp to find it burned to the ground and their families all taken captive. They wept until they had no strength left. David's men even began to talk of stoning him. The next verse was powerful to me. *David was greatly distressed because the men were talking of stoning him; each one was bitter in spirit because of his sons and daughters. But David found strength in the Lord his God* (1 Samuel 30:6, NIV).

David had to run to the Lord to get his focus right so he could continue to go on. God had called him to be king. God had been faithful to him in many, many circumstances. God was not through with David; He still had plans for him. No one could remove David from God's hand and God's plan for him. David began to act like the leader he had been called to be. God was enough. If everyone else was against him, God was for him. God was speaking into me that courage, in the midst of difficult places, and staying encouraged was a choice. God was bigger than all these circumstances! God was not finished with us. His plans could not be reversed.

Often the enemy uses fear to tempt us to run to other things or people. There are also times when God uses people or changes in circumstance to be His tool of provision or deliverance. However, running to Him must be our first step. When we go to the Lord, He brings truth and clarity. We are often called to obey and walk in faith when we are feeling fearful. We cannot always get rid of the feeling of fear, but we can refuse to allow it to control us. These are two different things. I went to the Lord with my fear, and He reminded me of how He had been leading us. *Lord, you have assigned me my portion and my cup; you have made my lot secure. The boundary lines have fallen for me in pleasant places; surely I have a delightful inheritance* (Psalm 16:5-6, NIV).

God reminded me that these were the very words my mother used to describe our home when she was living with us just before she passed away. She had said, "This is a very pleasant place." We were not in the habit of accumulating debt and that was scary to us. God said to us: *Do not be afraid to go down to Egypt… I will go down to Egypt with you, and I will surely bring you back again* (Genesis. 46:3-4, NIV). From Genesis 42, He had said to go to Egypt for grain and reminded us that even the grain (money) in Egypt belonged to Him. I had often regarded debt as Egypt. God reminded me that Egypt was sin when we run to any "Egypt" instead of Him. Abraham's going to Egypt was sin, yet God called Jacob, and many years later Mary and Joseph, to go to Egypt as His provision. *By wisdom a house is built, and through understanding it is established; through knowledge its rooms are filled with rare and beautiful treasures* (Proverbs 24: 3-4 NIV). We knew that those rare and beautiful treasures were the people God had given us to be in this house. He reminded us from verse 10 of the same chapter of Proverbs: *If you falter in times of trouble, how small is your strength!* From Psalms He said: *Trust in the Lord and do good; dwell in the land and enjoy safe pasture. Delight yourself in the Lord and he will give you the desires of your heart. Commit your way to the Lord; trust in him and he will do this: He will make your righteousness shine like the dawn, the justice of your cause like the noonday sun* (Psalms 37:3-6, NIV).

We were re-enforced in the Lord and ready to move ahead. One of the business team members asked me how we expected to pay for a mortgage since we could not pay the rent they were requiring. Our response was that the rent was not our debt. The mortgage would be our responsibility. God would provide. God reminded me that all these changes were totally unexpected to us, so we definitely could not expect others to comprehend this different and odd life of ours. The enemy would so love to use this for division and hard feelings. We couldn't allow that to happen. God was developing a heart for displayed unity within us. The dots continued to connect for the beautiful foundation that God was building for His ministry which was, at this time, still in the birthing stage!

When we were first approached about moving into the house which the businessmen purchased for our ministry, we'd had a concern that the house would not legally be ours, but there was nothing we could do about it. After the situation we had previously dealt with regarding our neighbor and landlord, we were uneasy. God had clearly directed us to move in this direction. We did so knowing that if we needed to be the owners of the house, God would work it out. From a place of spiritual warfare and the strongholds in the lives of many of those who would be living in our home, we believed our position would be much better as owners than simply residents. We once tried to discuss it with John, but he dismissed it without any consideration. We wanted our hearts to be right before the Lord and our motives pure, so we chose to trust the Lord and not push for what could be construed as our personal agenda. God went before us, and we were now the owners. This is not how we would have chosen things to work out, but God was in charge and we were fine. Our closing was mid-October and my journal was filled with the verses God had given me as we walked this road. Six weeks later, in December, we made our first house payment. We have never missed being able to pay the mortgage payments. What was impossible with man became possible with God. He is faithful! This became a great heritage for us as we began to build this ministry called WLFJ. We often found ourselves under the threat of someone more (seemingly) powerful than us, yet God prevailed for us, His little "dust people." *For he knows how weak we are; he remembers we are only dust* (Psalms 103:14, NLT). God continued to carefully fit the pieces together keeping us on His unseen path.

As WLFJ continued to grow, we had to develop computer generated spreadsheets to keep the ministry organized. Every day, a different group of people or churches came to one of the food locations to receive food, then the remainder was delivered to the community. A second grocery store heard about what we were doing and asked if we could collect their food as well. An interesting thing began to happen. Many mornings when I raised the garage doors, I found a piece of furniture or a few boxes of books, household items, or some other items sitting outside the doors. Folks in the community realized that outreach was taking place from this house and had begun dropping off donations. The same thing was happening at Kevin's home. Every couple of weeks, we placed a garage sale sign in the yard. We had to do this to keep our garage from being overrun with the accumulation. Trying to maintain order was a constant challenge. Folks seeing the yard sale signs would stop to shop. When they asked how much we wanted for something, we'd say, "Please receive this with love from Jesus." People did not know how to respond, but were always delighted to get something free. One day a lady stopped and asked the price for a book. We told her it was hers "with love from Jesus." She was blessed. A few hours later she returned and wrote us a check for one hundred dollars to support the work that God was doing in the community. We even received our first vehicle donation while working from the garage. We were able to absorb and use this car for the many delivery runs each day. Entenmann's Bakery donated food and also donated a work van. It needed engine work, but a local high school mechanics shop class took it on as a project and soon had it up and running. We bolted a seat in the back complete with seatbelts so children could ride in safety and help serve their neighbors. It was amazing to watch God at work.

When we received our first large financial donation of $1,000, we set the money aside knowing God must have sent it for a specific purpose. In May of 2002, after two years of running the ministry from the homes, we moved into our first warehouse paying $1,000 per month for the space on a month-to-month lease. The money we had set aside was the first month's rent and became our step of faith that God would continue to provide, and He did.

Once WLFJ moved into that first warehouse building in the spring of 2002, everything began to change and move quickly. That first facility was $1,000 a month for 8,000 square feet. We moved a couple of months later to the warehouse next door with the same landlord which was $2,000 per month for 12,000 square feet. We had been there only a couple of months when the owner told us he had someone willing to pay $5,000 per month for our space. Since we were on a month-to-month lease, he said we needed to move. We had hardly settled into this space and moving was not what we wanted to do. We were beginning to feel like a ministry of nomads, always on the move.

We sought wisdom from the Lord. God reminded us of our family's recent history of a mortgage payment that seemed foolish, yet He provided. He gave us peace to say we would pay the $5,000 as long as we were guaranteed a year's lease. Every month was a miracle. Once we were short $1,500 on the day the rent was due. In the mail was a check for $1,000 from a lady in Alaska that we had never met and another unexpected check for $500. Again the rent was paid. Another thing that happened during this year was that God spoke to Greg and Tara that Greg should quit his job to serve at WLFJ. Just as he had left the Navy when God directed, he stepped away from a full-time job with benefits to split his days between serving at WLFJ, helping with the home ministry, and joining Tara in homeschooling their children.

God was growing us and working in the community, too. Mary's story will forever be one of my favorites. She arrived at WLFJ looking for a refrigerator and was six months pregnant with twins. She and her husband had lost everything. They had borrowed someone's truck to come and see if we had a refrigerator. We had one refrigerator, but it had no shelves. She gladly received it. As it was being loaded onto a truck, a few of the volunteers gathered around Mary and asked God to bless her and to provide the shelves for that appliance. This was a Wednesday.

On Friday she returned to the ministry with a huge smile on her face. She shared with us the story of how she received the shelves. Mary said, "I received those shelves because you prayed."

I said, "No, Mary, you received those shelves because Jesus loves you!"

We sat together and I invited one of our new volunteers to join us. I shared with Mary how God wanted to reveal Himself to her and draw her to Himself. He wanted to be in the delivery room, He wanted to rebuild their lives, and He wanted to be involved in every area of their lives. After sharing the gospel, I asked Mary if she would like to receive Christ. We bowed our heads together. As I led prayer, I heard two voices crying out for salvation. On that day, Mary and the new volunteer both received Christ. Mary's great need and a donated refrigerator without shelves became just the right opportunity for God to build His Kingdom! We welcome volunteers who don't know Jesus to serve with us. Our desire is that the love of the Body experienced in the building, and the power of Holy Spirit God at work, will put within them a desire for what they witness. We have had teams of volunteers from other religious sects serve with us. We are wise in where they are placed and expectant that God will use their service as He woos them to Himself. Ministry most often comes through the public doors, but it sometimes comes to volunteers or donors.

At WLFJ we've witness God's multiplying act many times. One morning, in the early days of being in a building, Sam and I were working alone as we prepared for a new day of ministry. We realized that there was very little food to give away. We could hear the community beginning to assemble at the entrance door. We continued setting up for the day as we prayed for God's provision. It's one of the earliest memories I have of reminding God that this was His ministry, and He was the One who had called those people to assemble outside. This ministry was His idea! Whenever we are in a difficult or challenging circumstance, this is my go to place with God. He is gracious to allow us to cast our burdens on Him and gives us peace in knowing He has a plan. He had a plan for that day, too. A few minutes before we were to open, there was a bang at the loading dock door. We opened it to find a pickup truck loaded higher than a pickup truck should be loaded. It was filled with beautifully packaged fresh salads and boxes of apples. The driver said he worked at the nearby coliseum. They had realized that morning that all this food would expire before their next sporting event. Someone told them about this new little start-up ministry down the street, and they wanted to know if we could use it. All morning, as we served the community, we gave away beautiful grilled chicken salads. Each was packaged complete with the chicken in a sealed bag, cheese, croutons, dressings, and all the fixings to make a deluxe salad. Each family took home one per family member along with enough apples to bless their household. At the end of the day many families had been blessed and there was enough left over to feed our very large household as well. As we enjoyed our salads and cobbler made from the apples that night, there was overwhelming joy that we were sharing a meal with many in our community. The thing I know about that day is that we gave away more salads than would fit on that truck. God not only provided but also multiplied His provision.

As 2003 progressed and spring came, God began to speak to WLFJ leadership about moving to a spacious land, flowing with milk and honey. We were content where we were, but God continued to talk of moving. Our lease was coming to an end when the owner told us he was going to divide the 12,000 square feet into two sections. We could continue to rent half of the space, but it would still be $5,000 per month. Now we were ready to think about moving. God was talking about spacious land and our landlord was cutting our space in half. We chose not to sign a new lease. We had no idea what the next step would be, but knew God had a place—a spacious place.

At the end of August, as we were preparing to pack every-thing into the trailer of an eighteen-wheeler that was loaned to us, we were surprised by God again. Sam was on his way back from picking up chips from the Wise Potato Chip warehouse in south Raleigh when he pulled through an older shopping center. As he looked over that nearly empty shopping center, he knew that this shortcut was a God appointment and that this was where the ministry was going to move. He came back and shared his excitement with us. We jumped into vehicles and fol-lowed him to take a look. As soon as we saw the building, we knew it was where we were going. God gave us eyes to see what He was seeing because the physical building left much to be de-sired. It was gutted with no electricity, no dividing walls, and was terribly dusty. It was 116,000 square feet and definitely a spacious land. We called the leasing company to learn that Wal-Mart had a hold on the shopping center for a future location. It was not available to be rented. We could not shake the confi-dence that this was where we were going. We kept praying, looking, and seeking God's heart.

Everything was loaded into the trailer, and we went back to working from the garage and basement and hand delivering bags of groceries. This was difficult for us. As we went back to this old way of life, we were surprised by how much strength God had poured into us in the past to serve in this way. When we were in the community, we heard from those we were serv-ing how they missed being able to come and shop. Some were not aware that we were the same team who ran the building they were talking to us about. They just knew that there had been a place, and they missed it. It was as though we heard the community crying out for their own place to shop. We now had a team of volunteers that served regularly and helped lead the ministry. Each week, when our leadership team meet, we would bring our folding chairs and assemble under the front canopy of the building to pray and to plan the next week. The shopping center was so deserted that we were hardly noticed. It was like we were invisible, covered over by the hand of God. We would prayer-walk the shopping center each week. It seemed on the surface like a foolish thing to do, but we had confidence in how God had spoken. There was nothing else we knew to do but pray, so pray we did!

We met a brother in Christ, Mike, who actually worked for the leasing company for the shopping center. He wanted to help us find an affordable space for the ministry. After looking at many places, he found a warehouse building in the same vicinity. Kevin and I went to meet him there to sign a lease for the space. I had no peace about signing that lease, but nothing else was coming together. We didn't feel that we had any other options. I prayed all the way to the meeting that God would intervene or direct us. Our hearts were to honor Him. When we arrived at the meeting, Mike said that after talking to their insurance company, he could not lease the space to us. With tractor trailers pulling through this warehouse parking lot every day, it was too dangerous for us to have the public coming and going at the same time. I immediately had peace that this was God's protection over us. It's an amazing thing when you recognize that the God of the universe has intervened and actually stopped something that would be a mistake. I wanted a place to house the ministry, but I wanted God's place. In many ways the place that we were looking at was much nicer than what we wanted. Nicer was not better. It caused my mind to go back to the stable in Bethlehem. The Inn was certainly much nicer than the stable. The stable was more difficult, but it was God's choice and it was right. My friend Debbie Wilson, in her book *Little Women Big God* reminds us that the stable also provided privacy for Mary and Joseph to welcome the Holy Child without the intrusion of onlookers. It made an approachable place for their special guests to come and worship Jesus.

Then Mike said, "Have you considered that old Pak-n-Save building on Chapanoke?"

The breath went out of me as I told him that was the space we wanted.

He said, "Well, let's put you in that space."

God was providing. When we had inquired earlier from another realtor about the same space, he said it would lease for $58,000 per month if it was available. We, of course, knew this was not only unreasonable but also impossible. God had given us the figure of $5,000, and we did not have peace to go over that amount. Everything we looked at cost much more and nothing was convenient for those we served. Because the space was one large open area, Mike worked out a lease that gave us a few square feet in several different sections of the building. In reality, that gave us the entire space and the lease agreement came to $4,999 per month. We were delighted and signed that lease on October 15, 2003. Coming up with a first month's rent, deposit, and other fees was huge for us. Many people contributed to make it possible. On November first, two months after vacating our last building, we moved into this new spacious land.

Before leaving our previous facility, we were notified that a powdered milk grant we had applied for was approved. We had to give a delivery address for the numerous shipments to be delivered. As we approached the deadline date for the point of destination, there was no address to give them. Several truck loads were obviously too much for garages. Kevin and I agreed to give the address for the shopping center. It was our step of faith that God was working it out. A couple of days after moving into the new location, the trucks rolled in with huge shipments of milk. WLFJ was picking up large amounts of cookies, cakes, and other sweets from local grocery stores and outlets. We had moved into a spacious land, flowing with milk and "honey." It was another month-to-month lease situation. The leasing company said we could probably lease it for about eighteen months. Over the next few months, we received several milk grants. There were so many pallets of milk and milk products that we actually used them to make dividing walls in our building. WLFJ had a beautiful partnership with a local branch of Child Evangelism Fellowship. They offered little Bible Clubs for the children of our guests while they were shopping. With all this open space, it was difficult to contain the children. We used pallets of this milk to make a huge boxed-in area of the building to corral the children to keep them safe. God has a great sense of humor and very creative ideas. We could not afford to build walls, so He sent us portable walls in the form of milk.

Though the prison class was going strong and ladies were staying with us, we realized that the home ministry phase of our lives was coming to an end. The foster children and their mother continued to live with us until her intense parole ended. She was blessed with a great work-release job while incarcerated which continued after her release from prison. They soon moved into their own place. Other Bible study members came and went but most were only short term. Our focus was now primarily on this ministry that God had started as a surprise to all of us. We had seen God do this in the past. We would be busily doing the last thing He directed us to do when the path turned and a transition happened. God taught us as a family, and now as a ministry, that today's obedience paves the way for tomorrow's direction. As long as we were seeking Him and walking in an obedient love relationship with Him, He would not let us miss the next fork in the road. Though often unseen, His path is clear.

We never advertised that we were opening and this location was across the county from where we had previously been housed, yet on the first day, the people came. Sam and Greg worked to get electrical outlets run, lights on, and the walk-in cooler installed. It was a busy, exciting time. There were no restrooms in the building for our volunteers, but God gave us a lovely neighbor who shared with us. She had a thrift shop that was not doing well financially and seemed that it might be closing down any day. We prayed that as people came to us, they also visited her shop. There was no competition. We prayed for her business to grow and prosper. Her business did greatly increase, allowing her to stay open another year. We enjoyed a great relationship during that time. It was a beautiful display of unity! Once the thrift shop closed, Greg and Sam had completed enough of the other work that they could now move ahead with building restrooms.

In the spring of 2004, God told me that Kevin and Shelly were going to be called away from WLFJ and that I was to step into the role of director. I did not say anything to anyone as I tried to understand what was about to happen. It was taking me time to process this direction from the Lord. I did a lot of listening and praying during those weeks. Gradually peace grew in me and even a bit of expectancy. One day in late summer, Kevin asked if we could grab lunch together. He needed to share something with me. I knew what he was going to tell me. He said he and Shelly were being called away and asked if I would be willing to step into the role of director. The Lord had already prepared me for this step. Their plan was to give up their role at the end of 2004. We had been riding the waves of this new ministry now for four years, with Kevin and Shelly covering the role of co-directors for the past three. I was thankful God had given me time to process and prepare for this next step. We had been in the building nearly a year when we received a notice from the landlord that we needed to be out by the end of the year. Kevin came to me and said he was not prepared to move the ministry again. He was turning it over to me, effective immediately, to negotiate with the landlord, but would not officially step down until the end of the year. This was something I was not expecting!

It was late October with our busiest time of the year ahead of us. The great needs in the community became even greater at Christmas. I remembered well what life was like for us in years past when we were going through difficult financial times with Sam out of work and Christmas adding even more need. As a ministry we had two choices. We could either continue to serve the community through the end of the year and focus on their needs, or start packing up and looking for another place. I called the landlord and asked if we could negotiate around this deadline, explaining to him the huge needs of our community. He seemed indifferent to my plea. As a team, we made the decision to serve the community as we continued to pray. A friend of the ministry with a media position wrote a story about the struggles of our ministry as we tried to serve the community under the threat of eviction by the landlord. The media quickly jumped on the story and interviewed us and tried to interview the property owner. They never received an interview with the owner or his agent, but he backed down. We continued to pay the rent each month, and he continued to accept it. The eviction deadline came and went and we were continuing to serve the community. We later learned that the contract with Wal-Mart had fallen through. Over the next eighteen months, there were several contracts on the shopping center and several eviction notices, but nothing ever materialized. Each time we received a notice, we sought God's direction. He always directed us to continue paying the lease. We paid it. The landlord kept it. It seemed that we worked daily under the threat of having to close down, however we were enjoying God's favor and His provision in what felt like the constant presence of our enemy.

Another unexpected thing happened during this time. My dad called me a few days before Christmas to ask if I would take him to the doctor. He was feeling unusually weak and knew something was not right. He was seriously ill. Over the next weeks, he was in and out of the hospital many times before he passed away. I was dependent on the Lord to show me each day what I needed to do. I would be at the ministry and Holy Spirit God would nudge me to put my work aside and go to the hospital. Or, I might be at the hospital with Dad and God would release me to go back to the ministry. This went on for weeks. The days seemed a bit like a juggling act, but the Lord's presence was real and personal. I, again, learned during those days that I can lead a ministry and care for family and not compromise in either place. It was a beautiful time for my dad and me (my mom had passed away five years earlier). He and I had many Kingdom conversations. He also knew I was in a new place of leadership. He loved advising me from his years of business experience. It seemed like crazy timing to me. In looking back, I can clearly see God's perfect involvement. My attention being divided between the ministry at WLFJ and the ministry into my dad's final days was perfect.

I, again, received great emotional support from my brother. He was always quick to take my phone calls and helped me think through many decisions that we had to make for our dad. Every day, Dad's situation was changing along with his care needs. My sister was struggling and could not bring herself to come to the hospital to visit him. The hardest part for me was trying to console Dad that she loved him, but was in a difficult emotional place. My heart ached for them both. Her pain was real. His was, too! When I called her from the hospital the day he died, she cried in disbelief. I think she had convinced herself that he was not that seriously ill. In the days ahead she rode a rollercoaster of anger and regret. It hurt to see her stuck in a place of her own choice as she refused to get the help she needed. There are times at WLFJ when we witness the pain in greatly dysfunctional families as they continue to make life choices which keep them bound, when they could have freedom. It is a constant reminder, that as we walk planet earth, no family is exempt from pain and struggles. We all have to depend on God to cover and redeem many things. There are no perfect families.

In the days before my dad passed away, I saw the evidence in his life that he had received Christ. He never told me with his own words, but his deep interest in the Lord and prayer (and always wanting me to pray with him) revealed a new nature. After he was gone, I was challenged for days as the enemy tried to serve up to me that I was wrong. I walked in the truth even as the battle was raging. One night the Lord gave me forever relief from the taunts. He gave me an amazing dream. I was seated at a long, never-ending table. I was laughing and talking to people and got up to go to the buffet table to fix a plate of food. As I approached the table, I saw the back of a man who was wearing a shirt like my dad's favorite shirt. The man was carrying a plate piled high with every kind of seafood (my dad's favorite food). My eyes could not leave him. He looked like a younger, stronger version of my dad. I slowly approached him, reached out, and touched his arm. It was strong and muscular. Dad's arms had lost their muscle mass years earlier. As I touched him, he turned and looked at me. It was my dad! He had an amazing smile on his face and a twinkle in his eyes that seemed to say, "I made it." Never again would the enemy be able to use those taunts against me.

In this new role of director, God took me to the book of Joshua. He said to me that Moses (former director) was gone, so I needed to focus on exactly what He told me to do. I was not to be fearful. I had to be courageous, and I could not let myself get discouraged. Meditating on His Word day and night would keep me focused and would help prevent me from becoming discouraged. Meditating on His Word could mean studying the Bible, but it could also mean declaring and proclaiming the things He had said to me and the promises He had made to me. In John 14, He instructed his disciples not to be troubled. In Lamentations 3, He gives a prescription to take if we see ourselves getting discouraged. We are called to *remember*. Remembering what He has done, remembering what He has said, and praising Him for who He is and how He has worked, had to be part of my daily life. He told me to never stop praising Him and He would take care of the rest. God told me that the transition of leadership was a small part of what was happening. God was taking us to a new level of ministry, and He was unfolding His path before us. Staying close to Him was the answer!

The ministry was growing with resources flowing into the building. We were also seeing increasing numbers of shoppers. God reminded me of the verses that He had given our family years ago. *I was hungry and you gave me something to eat* (Matthew 25:35, NIV). Jesus identified Himself as the one in need. This thought played repeatedly in my mind. We began to look at those who came to be served as Jesus Himself coming to our door. We no longer referred to those who came to receive resources as shoppers. They became our honored guests. On the outside, the ministry probably did not appear any different. It was interesting to observe how this new focus made a difference in us. Looking with expectancy for Jesus to show up each day gave fresh vision. We spoke over our visitors that they were honored guests, and that declaration made a difference as well. We saw the community rise up under that title in two very different ways. In one way, it spoke value and honor. In another, it carried folks from a mindset of entitlement, to the privilege of being invited to receive. Once, we had an honored guest get enraged with us about something. I have long ago forgotten the details of her grievance, but will never forgot how God worked through it. She called the police on us. I listened with interest as the officer explained to her that we had invited her in as our guest so we could also ask her to leave. We did not charge her a fee and did not ask anything from her, so we could limit whatever we chose to limit. It was our gift to her and not her right. The officer looked at me and asked if I wanted to press charges against her. I explained that I did not call him and I had nothing against her. She melted with tears into my arms. I encouraged her to leave that day because she had caused quite a scene, but told her to feel free to come back at another time. The policeman looked at her and said, "I would not have advised her to go this route. You are very lucky." God was at work and had us on His training ground.

Another change in perspective came as I was praying one morning about the daily crowds coming to the building. I saw the fields white with harvest. The Lord spoke to me that the harvest was not the crowd, but was *in* the crowd. Jesus fed the crowds. Jesus spoke into the crowds and sometimes even healed great numbers. Jesus had the crowds pushing in on Him daily, yet He was quick to see the one in the busy crowd that was truly seeking Him. A blind man, the woman who had been bleeding for twelve years, Jarius' daughter, the centurion's servant, the demon-possessed man, the leprous man, and many others, were the harvest in the midst of the crowds. We were called to feed all that came, and to share the Word with all, but Jesus had us begin to look for the harvest in the crowd. We looked for that one that responded to the gospel message, or asked for prayer, or had questions, to see if these might be places we should minister on a deeper level. I was also impressed that Jesus always controlled the crowds. He never allowed the crowds to control Him. We cried out to the Lord for Him to show us how to maintain that position in His house at WLFJ. He has given us many ways to better facilitate the crowd, which accomplishes His purposes, and is a blessing to those whom we serve. Crowd control for Jesus was never angry or disrespectful. He daily showed us His ways to manage the crowds in an attitude and atmosphere of respect and honor.

One problem that we constantly dealt with was people arriving very early and forming long lines in the parking lot. It is a habit built by many in need who go to local government agencies for help. Arriving early would often better guarantee that they'd be served. It was important to us to set a different standard. God can be trusted, and learning to rest in Him for His provision was an important truth we wanted our community to learn. Folks with great needs standing in long lines presented too many opportunities for the enemy to work. Our neighboring businesses were inconvenienced by this situation as well. God gave us a plan. We made our first group of the day a food only group. If folks wanted food only, they arrived between 9:30 and 10:00. Guests arriving after 10:00 were invited to shop for household items, clothing, shoes, and furniture as well as food. This limited those that came early because most wanted the option to shop the full building. We took a firm stand on not allowing folks to arrive prior to 9:30. With the smaller numbers to deal with now, this was easier to enforce. It totally solved the issue without causing problems with the community and our neighbors. God was faithful to give us a simple but successful solution. At first the community struggled with this plan, but soon it became routine. If a guest arrived for the first time before 10:00, they were welcomed in to shop for food and explained the policy. We told them that this was their day to learn how we operated, and they could choose in the future which group they preferred. We always encouraged our honored guests that the choice was theirs. The time they chose to arrive decided the resources they would like to receive. It was freeing for us, and has become a place of blessing for the community, too. We have folks that purposefully come at 9:30 or a few minutes prior to 10:00 because they only need food. They want to get in and out quickly. This is the perfect group for them. For people with food needs, who also have job or family obligations, this is a great service. It is God's way to use even these standards to broaden places of blessing for our neighbors. We are amazed at God's wisdom. We have none, but He is generous to share His wisdom with us as we ask Him.

There are times when donors or others inquiring about the ministry ask how we keep the community from being dependent on us. It is simple. We do not try to be their solution or cure. We give people enough resources to bless them and to be a help. We welcome them to come each week, but they do not receive enough from us to support their family. We constantly turn their eyes to the real Supplier. As Jesus fed the crowds, so do we. As Jesus looked for those that wanted to turn their need into relationship, so do we. Our strategy is to follow Him!

Chapter 10
Keeping in Step

*And when we obey him, every path he guides us on is fragrant with
his loving-kindness and his truth.*
Psalm 25:10, Living Bible

He has taught us to keep Him and His ways in all that we do.
Many times we knew that the food or other resources should
have run out, but they did not. Every person received a provision from the Lord. God reminds us in Mark 8 how Jesus gave
thanks for the fish and bread and directed His disciples to pass
out the food right away. He did not wait to see it multiply before
He started feeding the crowds. We take what we are given and,
with thankful hearts, begin to serve the community. Once we ran
out of meat with the first group of the day. As people continued
to come in to be served, a truck pulled up to the loading dock
and off-loaded cases of frozen lasagna. The portions were huge.
All of our guests were delighted with their meal and no one had
to worry that we were out of meat. Another day we had only
enough household items to serve about forty people. We were
expecting more than two hundred guests. We brought in our

honored guests and began to serve them. A phone call came in from one of our partners indicating they had a large supply of toiletry items that needed to be passed along to free up space. A volunteer drove to the other ministry and loaded our truck. Within forty-five minutes, and before we had given away our current supply, volunteers were unloading wonderful treasures to give to our guests as their household item. Every day, donations are dropped off at the loading dock door by folks and those resources become evangelism tools that grant us the opportunity to share Jesus with our neighbors. It's amazing to see how someone's gently used extra can become an essential provision for someone else. Whether it's dishes, linens, paper goods, hygiene items, or a piece of furniture, there is someone in our community who needs it. We never know exactly what we will have to give away, but God always makes it work. He is the same God today that He has always been. Amazing God!

As we continued to walk with the Lord, learning His ways to better minister to the community, we had our family to care for as well. One Saturday morning in August of 2006, I was in the building preparing for a busy day when I received a phone call from my sister's husband. They were going through difficult times, and he had chosen to temporarily move out and stay with their son. In the past, she would have called him nearly constantly. This time seemed strange. She had not tried to call him for several days. She was not emotionally or physically well. He had tried to call their home, but she did not answer and he was anxious. I called their home and left a message for her on the answering machine. Usually, she would have called me back right away, but I didn't hear a word. Her husband called again to say he was asking the police to check on her. A few minutes later, I received a call from him saying that the police had checked their house and told him he needed to come home immediately. He had jumped in his truck to drive home and wanted me to meet him there. Volunteers were coming in and my day was already full and busy. God had gone before me because there was an experienced volunteer serving with me that I could leave in charge. Sam and I rushed to our van and headed to my sister's house which was a little over an hour away. We arrived to find that she had died about twenty-four hours earlier. When you walk through life with someone you love, and you hunger for them to get help and to have a better life, you always dream of the day when all will be better. The day that we had hoped for would not come on this earth. For days we thought she had taken her life. After receiving the medical report, we learned that she died from an illness that could have been cured had she been willing to receive help. I had peace that her suffering was over. She was with the Lord and our parents. I would enjoy spending eternity with her without the baggage that made her earthly life so unbearable at times. However, God is still our redeemer even in this. A few days after her death, Greg gave the message at WLFJ. He shared her story, and as a result, one lady went to the prayer center and asked for help to receive Christ. Two others sought the Lord for forgiveness and made a new commitment to the Lord. It's never too late for God to bring blessing out of pain and destruction. From her heavenly position, I'm sure my sister is blessed, too!

* * *

The battles with the landlord continued and we faced many fire marshal issues as well. God spoke to several of us in leadership from Psalm 37:34. From the Living Bible we read: *Don't be impatient for the Lord to act! Travel steadily along His path. He will honor you, giving you the land. You will see the wicked destroyed.* It was obvious to us that our landlord was a tool being used by the enemy for wicked purposes. We became more and more expectant to see how God would resolve this issue for us.

At one point, the landlord was pressing us to leave. We were seeking God and had no direction to move. We became aware of a piece of property near our current building that was for sale. It was a good size for the ministry, so we prayed about the property and had peace to pursue it. We began negotiations with the owner, and an interesting thing happened as we walked this road. I called our current landlord and asked if he could give us a little extension in time to make an offer for the purchase of another building. It appeared that he was content to leave us alone as long as we were negotiating on another piece of property. It was as though he could be patient for a while knowing that he would soon be rid of us. The situation with the media a year or so earlier seemed to cause him to want to make this happen without incident. We made an offer and it was countered by the owner. We made a counter offer. Back and forth it went for months. It was obvious after a time that this was God's stalling plan with our landlord. Eventually, we had to walk away from it. We had a promise of receiving the shopping center and knew that God could bring us back if we moved, but had no sense that a move would ever take place. However, this endeavor bought us months of peace with the current owner. God truly works in many different ways. His tools are unlimited.

We were constantly seeking God's heart and asking Him to reveal to us anything He wanted us to learn or any place that we might be out of step with Him. He revealed nothing to us that needed to be changed, yet another eviction notice arrived. According to the owner there was a contract on the building and the new owner would not close until we were out of the space that we currently occupied. We pursued every possible lead to find out who was buying the building but kept coming up with dead ends. God was telling us one thing and the landlord was telling us something else. God reminded me of another time and place for our family, when God was clearly calling us to take in prisoners yet our church and landlord said no. God's plan would prevail now as it had then. God was up to something, and we had learned to trust Him. In the days to come, two different pastors came to me and shared that their church had once been in this shopping center and believed God was going to give them the shopping center. They had prayer-walked the land many times. The unreasonableness of the landlord eventually wore them down and both churches moved to another location. The pastors said that, in time, they came to realize that the move had been a mistake. One pastor told me that by the time they moved into their new building, they were sad they had given up. Both exhorted us not to give in to the pressures of the owner. We were encouraged, but still didn't know our next step.

Walking in close intimacy with God would be our solution. When we first moved to this location, the sign was ordered for the front of our building. We had come to be known as the With Love From Jesus Community Resource Center. Somehow along the way, resource center had been tacked on to our name. The first morning when I arrived at the building to find the new sign in place, I was taken aback with disappointment. In huge letters the sign read *Resource Center*. In very small print contained in a little square were the words *With Love From Jesus*. I remember looking at the sign in disbelief. I'm not sure to this day how that happened. Did the sign company make a mistake or did the person placing the order make a mistake? The money was spent. The sign was up. A reporter called to do a story on the ministry, and when he came to do the report, he asked if we were called Community Resource Center or With Love From Jesus. He made the comment that it couldn't be both. I took this remark to the Lord later that night as I reflected on the interview. God directed us to take Community Resource Center off our sign. I discussed it with the Board and all agreed. Keith, one of our board members, spent hours carefully pulling the resource center letters off the building and re-making the sign with a large *With Love From Jesus Ministries* in its place. God wanted His name boldly on His shopping center. He wanted no compromise. Jesus is our name. We cannot pull away from this for any reason. There are times that we miss getting grants because Jesus is in our name. We gladly give up the grant in order to boldly declare the name of Jesus. Since then, the shopping center has been remodeled and our area is a different place, so that sign has now come down. However, high on the marquee in front of the shopping center is our name *With Love From Jesus.*

We decided to have a night of worship in the building and invited a praise team to come in and lead us in worship and in seeking God's help. It was a great—yet odd—night in many ways. The group took many outside of their comfort zone, but we recognized that God was at work in the evening. Their style of worship was different than we had expected, but we had invited them and believed God was in the evening. That night someone on the worship team came to me and said that we were going to meet a man that would change everything for us.

The next day I was alone working in the building when I realized we were out of some things we needed for the next day. I jumped in my car to run to the store to buy the supplies and, as I was backing out, I saw a man standing in the middle of the empty parking lot.

The Lord said to me, "That is the new owner."

I pulled my car over to where he was standing and asked if I could help him.

He said, "Are you Linda?"

It was obvious that the landlord had told him about me. He said he was the new owner, but since the closing had not happened yet, he couldn't come in without the consent of the current owner. I asked him if he would like to come in and look around. I had received a termination of lease notice, but I still had two months before I had to be out so I invited him in as my guest. He came in and walked around and asked what we did. I explained to him about WLFJ. He listened, but he told me that he had already rented the space we were in to someone else effective as soon as he closed on the purchase. I told him he was welcome to come anytime during the next two months and that he could bring anyone with him. I assured him that we considered him our guest, and he didn't need permission from the current landlord to come.

He took me up on my offer. Over the next two months, he often brought folks in to look around and discuss things. He was always pleasant and thanked me for allowing him to come in, but was careful not to ever give me his name. One day the current landlord's attorney came to visit us. She looked around and was annoyed that we were not packing to leave. Our deadline was just a few days away and she warned us that if we were not out, the doors would be padlocked. We felt foolish, but I am quite sure the children of Israel felt foolish marching around the walls of Jericho. There was really no way that we could possibly pack up and be out in the designated time. The Lord continued to tell us to stay and to keep ministering. The business agent for the owner had also come to see me a few weeks earlier and asked if we had found a new place to move. He wrote us a personal check for $1,000 and tried to give it to me as an incentive to leave earlier. I refused the check. The days were ticking by quickly, but we serve a Sovereign God and know His plans and purposes always prevail. We had to rest in that truth. A few days before we were to be out, the new owner came in with some of his partners. I went to him and asked if he could do anything to help us. He reminded me that our space was already rented and he was not sure if he had any other place he could lease to us. Our hope was in the Lord and not in this kind businessman, however, we did believe he was the man God had spoken to us about who would change our situation. Our eyes were firmly on the Lord.

Twenty-four hours before our scheduled eviction, the new owner came back with more people. On that day, as he entered the building, he asked questions about what we did and what our needs were. I once again asked him if there was anything he could do to help us He said to me, "Don't be upset with your landlord. He's just a company man. He has no authority." Then he said, "But I am not a company man. I will take care of the current owner for you, and I will find a place in the building to lease to you." We never again heard from the current owner or his agent. It took three more months for the purchase to close and during that time the current owner would not accept our lease checks. Each month we mailed them, and each month he sent them back. We saved the money knowing the new owner could not accept them until the sale was final. On the day of the closing, the new owner gave me a printout that showed that we were three months delinquent in paying the rent. I told him that we had tried, but it was refused. That day I gave him a check for the three months' rent. It was a pleasure to give him that check. Over the next several months, the new owner had us move around in the building several times while trying to find a spot for us.

The constant moving was difficult and presented us with many challenges because moving our operation was not a small thing. One day we were running outlets for the new area when he told us we were going to move to another place in the building. I couldn't tell the volunteer doing the wiring that he had to stop. He had worked too hard on this project. I thanked the owner, but we kept on settling into the current space. It turned out that we were able to stay there for a few months before we had to move again. It was strange, but being inconvenienced by this new owner was no big deal in comparison to the constant threat of eviction that we had been under with our former landlord. We had a confidence that this landlord was for us, and though moving was inconvenient, his heart was to bless us. During these months of transition, we worked hard at not allowing our moves to impact the community any more than it had to. Sometimes it meant we had to modify what we could do, but we were always open. Even as the owner's construction crew was at work on their huge remodel, they worked hard with us to make sure our honored guests were able to have an entrance so they could be served. The new owner was pleased that we were serving the community. Finally, we were allocated our own permanent space in the building with a two-year lease. When that lease was up, we signed a long-term lease. God allowed us to see "the wicked destroyed." We wait with great expectancy for the day that the shopping center will be ours. In the meantime, we continue to walk a path laid out before us by the King of Glory. He has given us Himself, Holy Spirit God, to walk with us and help us stay on the sometimes very narrow path.

WLFJ continues to be needy before our great and amazing God, for Him to work and direct us as days turn into months, and months quickly become years. In 2010, Troy was added to our staff as Director of Outreach. Responsibilities continue to grow and more people are needed to shoulder the broader outreach. We are thankful for the greater Body of Christ.

God began to move our hearts to take care of the name He had given for this ministry. There have been many inquiries from people interested in starting a WLFJ in their community.

This is exciting to us as a board but also a greater stewardship. God gave us His standards and in 2011, we applied for and received the trademark (service mark) for the ministry. Shortly thereafter an interesting situation came up.

Three brothers in Christ who were totally unconnected to each other came to me to ask about the ministry expanding into an adjoining county. We had many guests who traveled to us from Johnston County, so it seemed natural to begin a work there. I introduced the guys to each other and began to have meetings to discuss a ministry in that community. Each time we met, I would suggest the next action step needed to begin the outreach. Each time, they expressed their desire that it not be a new outreach, but an extension of the current ministry. A few weeks passed and we met again. This went on for several months. I kept encouraging them to start a ministry and they continued to express their desire that it be part of the existing ministry. Sam and I had been away for a few days with our family for a beach getaway. As just the two of us drove home together, I expressed to him my concern that the Johnston County outreach was not going to come together.

I said to him, "The guys want the ministry to happen but there seems to be no true understanding of the vision for displayed unity. It is as though that piece of the puzzle is always missing." His response took me to a different place.

He said, "Honey, it's because you hold that piece of the puzzle."

For the next several miles we traveled in total silence. In those miles, God the Holy Spirit began to speak to my heart. The conversation was as clear as if He was audibly speaking in the car. The Johnston County outreach was to be part of the Raleigh ministry. It was not supposed to be under a new ministry using the WLFJ trademark. I was stunned. This was not what I expected.

When I turned and looked at Sam, he said, "Where have you been? You left the car. What did God say to you?"

Sam knows me well. As I began to share with him, he quietly listened as he nodded his affirmation. We were going to expand into Johnston County.

In the days that followed, I spent long periods with the Lord trying to absorb this information. I asked the board for a special meeting to share with them the events of the past few days. As we met, the Lord confirmed to them this was our next step. A few months later, at another board meeting, we again sought the Lord for confirmation because there were no funds to take this step. The board had to be sure God had spoken before we could move ahead. God was gracious to confirm again to us that this was His plan.

Over the next few weeks, I looked for existing contacts in this new area that would help us begin to build. I also sought clarity for leadership in the next step. God gave us that clarity as I fellowshipped with some of the churches that were currently partnering with us from that area. In 2013, we established two satellites in Johnston County using two of our church partners. Each church allowed us to use their building to begin to serve our Johnston County neighbors. My son-in-law, Greg, and I worked together to get these outreach locations up and running. It was a fun, new, unexpected, and often challenging time. We developed new teams of volunteers to load and deliver resources into these new areas and help with set up and tear down. Volunteers served those who came to the satellites and whatever was leftover was made up into bags and delivered to the surrounding community. It reminded us of the old garage days more than ten years earlier. After more than a year of serving from the partnering churches, God provided for our first start-up building. We continue to walk a road not knowing the next step, but knowing the One who is leading us. He has not left us alone. There have been many adventures along the path with many more to come. "Thank you Jesus."

Chapter 11
Adventures Along the Path

*But giving thanks is a sacrifice that truly honors me. If you keep to
my path, I will reveal to you the salvation of God.*
Psalm 50:23, NLT

As we dealt with the landlord and other difficult issues, God
was also at work enabling us to bless our community. I looked
into the eyes of honored guests and felt their pain as I remembered challenges from our own family's past and remembered
how God had worked for us. Holidays are always difficult for
families in need. For our family, there had been many times in
which God had provided in unusual ways.

At WLFJ, we do not require people to prove they have needs.
If they show up at the door, they are welcome to come in and be
served. Our philosophy is that if you do not have Jesus, you are
poor. If you have Jesus, you can still have needs, but you are not
poor. Both are welcome! We had learned this and so much more
walking our path as a family. We were often without funds, but
we were never poor. Jesus' children are not beggars. They are
sustained by the King of Glory.

We are thankful to serve our brothers and sisters in Christ. Because our vision is to be a platform to display the unity of the Body of Christ, taking care of the Body is important to us. We understand from our family history that believers often go through difficult times. Sometimes God is bringing correction in our lives and sometimes He has us on His training ground.

Tamika and her roommate, who were both believers, came to the prayer center for prayer. A neighbor of theirs had been evicted and had left her apartment, but also left behind four small children. Tamika and her roommate had befriended the family and had taken time to get to know the children. When the children were deserted, they immediately stepped in to care for them. Tamika had been to social services and filed all the paperwork to receive legal custody for the precious children. It was our great pleasure to help them get beds and other things necessary for them to be able to step into this unexpected ministry role. We have had other people in ministry that were trying to either establish a church or a young ministry who find themselves in a place of need. When people lose jobs or sickness occurs, the Body needs to take care of the Body. It is our privilege to serve children of the King of Glory as they walk their own path with the Lord.

We find the assurance of God's provision for His own as we look at His Word. If we seek Him and His Kingdom and walk rightly before Him, He has promised that all else that we need will be provided. Sometimes we need to have a need, because our greatest need is to see Jesus show up in our lives. Often need opens our eyes to see God and gives us the opportunity to draw closer to Him. How sad it is to feel that we never have a need. Need can actually be a gift from God, an invitation to see Him work as we get to know Him in a better in a deeper place of intimacy. Where we can get into trouble is if we run to something or someone else instead of God when need presents itself. When God stepped into my life, I was riddled with need and looking in all the wrong places to get it met. I cannot imagine—it's scary to imagine—where I would be today had He not used need as an opportunity to draw me to Himself! "Thank you Jesus!"

God's faithfulness to us over many Christmases became another connecting dot to WLFJ. This connecting dot is called "The Jesus Shop." When our honored guests are preparing Christmas for their families, we look for ways to help them. There is a little section of the building that is set up during Christmas and supplied with only new toys. There is a specific week that we set aside for this fun little shop. As guests come to receive their food and other resources, they are given a ticket. Only adults are allowed to enter the Jesus Shop. Children stay outside under the watchful eye of a friend or another guest. The moms and dads are invited to receive some new things to help with their Christmas preparations. Everything is loaded into huge black trash bags, out of the children's view. It gives parents the ability to give their children surprises for Christmas. It is important to these parents that these gifts are from them, that they have shopped for them and picked them out for their children. We want to be a part of helping families establish their own traditions and nice memories. These gifts are given 'with love from Jesus' to the parents. This week is a highlight for many donors, volunteers, and parents in our community. I believe that one reason the Jesus Shop is so special to the community is because parents are empowered to be givers instead of having someone simply meet their children's Christmas wish list. The miracle of being a giver is important to everyone, but especially to parents.

The Lord reminded me of this recently as I was reading an old journal about a special Christmas, which seemed sparse from the perspective of Christmas gifts, but was rich with memories. The girls were older and the gifts under the tree were small. However, I had recorded in my journal the fun we shared together as we prepared gift bags for the ladies in the prison class. That year we also provided snack bags for the guys in the men's prison class. Our family went together to the prison on Christmas Eve and brought homemade goodies to serve as we sang Christmas Carols together. We had a huge tree that year which we had to secure with a cord to the wall to keep it from falling. How much fun we had trimming that tree together! So often the gifts under the tree are long forgotten, but the family traditions remain with us forever. Our Christmases were rich in memories. Some years there were big gifts like bicycles or new clothes, but every Christmas was special in Jesus and in family memories and traditions. Just as our heritage is filled with beautiful memories of God showing up for us, it was important to me that our honored guests at WLFJ have the same experience. We not only want to help provide goodies under their tree, but also want to help our guests understand that if they have Jesus, Christmas—and life—is wonderful.

The stories seem endless as God consistently shows up to display His glory through this simple little shop. It was the last day of the Jesus Shop and a couple arrived who had never shopped with us before. Someone in the community had told them about WLFJ, so they had come looking for Christmas gifts for their children. A volunteer encouraged them to stop in the prayer center. The prayer center volunteer chatted with them and shared the gospel. Whether it was the first time they'd heard it or the hundredth time, it was this time when it clicked for them. They both cried out for forgiveness of sins and asked Jesus for His salvation. The volunteer slipped tickets to the Jesus Shop into their hands. Their countenance shone with the radiance of changed hearts. We stood and marveled at God's work in their lives. He not only used the Jesus Shop to provide toys for their children's Christmas, but also used it to give this family a new life!

On another occasion, it was again the last group of the day to shop and these were our last guests to receive tickets for the Jesus Shop. We counted the toys and knew what we were able to handle with this last group. However, there were a few more guests than we had anticipated. We prayed for God to multiply the toys. We handed out tickets to all the guests knowing that God had a plan. A donor pulled into the loading dock with a small donation of toys which included a little red bicycle. About half-way through the day, we slipped the bicycle into the Jesus Shop. Angie spied the little red bike saying, "I know a child that needs that bike." Angie's children were grown, but she, her husband, and their twenty-four-year-old daughter were living in a low-rent motel in a bad area of town where the room beside theirs housed a young couple with a small child and one on the way. This young family was barely surviving and had no funds to buy a gift for their little daughter. Angie had never shopped with us and was new in town. Someone in the motel had told her about WLFJ. Her husband had planned to bring her to shop but was offered a job for the day and desperately needed the work. Angie decided to take the bus and figure out where we were because her family needed food and had no money. When she got on the bus, the driver told her she needed to transfer to another bus to reach our address. She made the transfer, but still did not know where she was going. She asked another rider on the bus if he knew about a place called With Love From Jesus. He was a regular guest on his way to shop so he led her to our door.

Now Angie had a little red bike, bags of groceries and clothes, and had to ride the bus including one transfer to return her to the motel. A volunteer graciously offered to give her a ride which made Angie very excited. She had used her ticket to bless someone else for Christmas. Not only had she received food and clothing for her family, but was also empowered to be a giver. What a blessing! She was thrilled!

At WLFJ we love watching God connect specific items with the family that should receive them. Victoria stopped in the prayer center seeking prayer for something she could give her four little girls together for Christmas. Victoria was dealing with cancer and the children were constantly under foot and her patience was stretched. She wanted an outside toy that would be a treat for them, but would also give her some alone time. A donor had given a huge plastic playhouse which we had set aside knowing God would show us exactly where it should go. Victoria's family was the perfect place. We were as thrilled as Victoria with God's timely provision for her and her children.

Jamie's young daughter had been in and out of the hospital for weeks. Her twelve-year-old son had shouldered much of the responsibilities at home, which included caring for younger brothers and sisters while she was away. She wanted something special to give him for Christmas. A volunteer purchased a nice remote control truck and asked that we look for the right child to receive it. Jamie's son was the child God had in mind when He prompted this volunteer to shop. It was an encouragement to Jamie to be able to surprise her son with this perfect and special gift for him.

The mom of a teenage daughter named Camilla was delighted when she found a beautiful new necklace in the Jesus Shop with the initial "C." Another mom danced with joy as she placed a skateboard in her big black bag. A mother stopped in the prayer center looking for pants for her son. His size was difficult for her to find. The volunteer prayed over the need while the mom moved on to do her other shopping. The volunteer went to our processing area and there were two new pairs of pants in that size hanging on the rack ready to be given away. Both mother and volunteer praised the Lord for His provision.

Over many years, I've observed that little extras can sometimes mean so much to families in difficult places. A shopping cart filled with bubbles or other small toys, pushed around the building by a volunteer who hands these treats out to children, can become great places of encouragement for families that do not have the ability to treat their children. Frozen popsicles handed out on a hot summer day or zippy bags filled with hotel samples can speak the love of Christ into the lives of our honored guests. Change left in a donated purse or a gift card with a small balance on it left in the pocket of a pair of jeans can become a treasure to someone with many needs. One donor with a homemade soap business gives the small trimmings from their soap-making. Bagged up and slipped into the pocket of clothing or into a bag with other items, these treats become the fragrance of Jesus to our neighbors.

One winter morning at WLFJ, we watched God turn a seemingly little thing into a big encouragement for many. It was a rainy February day and the building was cold but outside was much colder! A volunteer discovered a box brimming full with new gloves in all sizes. She stood at the checkout line as people gathered their treasures to take home and offered guests a pair of warm, new gloves to wear out into the cold rainy day. What a timely gift this was for cold hands!

At WLFJ we see needs every day turn into appointments with God. We almost never give funds to a guest, except for occasional bus fare. If a guest asks for help in paying a utility bill or rent, we have them tell their pastor to give us a call. Together with their pastor we try to find a way to help. If the guest does not have a church, we encourage them to go to a church, explain their need, and then have the pastor of that church give us a call. Often WLFJ is able to give the church the funds to equip them to cover the need. Our desire is to help our guests get engaged in a church for discipleship, growth, and accountability. WLFJ is not a church. We are here to serve and sometimes help equip the church to disciple some of their struggling members. Together we are a team.

Kelly came to WLFJ looking for financial assistance. She had recently started attending a local church but was not yet a believer. We had her contact the pastor and tell him to give us a call. We shared with him our heart to help her better connect with his church. Together we prayed for Kelly's salvation. WLFJ sent a check to the church to help cover part of Kelly's rent. The pastor led her to the Lord. A few months later, Kelly brought her friend, Sylvia, to WLFJ requesting prayer for a financial crisis. Again, we explained the need to hear from a pastor on her behalf. Kelly invited Sylvia to church the following Sunday. The pastor prayed for her and Sylvia received Christ. WLFJ provided a check to cover a portion of Sylvia's electricity bill and her new church covered the remainder. Praise God for the Body of Christ. How we praise Him for needs that lead to salvation. Our prayer is that one day our honored guests will look back at their time of need and crisis and give praise to God for how it became their entrance into the family of God!

To our honored guests, it must seem that WLFJ has no needs. What they do not know is that there are times when we have no idea how we will cover the growing financial needs of this ministry. Even as I am writing this manuscript, two churches who have been giving for years have found themselves in hard places and have notified us that they will no longer be able to help support the work at WLFJ. It is in these times that we have to keep the focus that God is our sustainer. His resources are beyond our ability to comprehend. Like the community that we serve, our eyes must stay on the Lord if we expect to make it in this difficult time on planet Earth.

God at work among our guests and volunteers, including miracles and healings, is part of the culture at WLFJ. I have witnessed and experienced this work and my heart cries out for more. When ministering to a large number of the un-churched community, it is interesting to see how God will show up in someone's life to reveal Himself to them. It could be a Spanish-speaking mom who places her feverish baby in your arms and looks helplessly for assistance. She cannot even communicate her need, nor does she have the resources to go to a doctor. Your heart cries for Jesus to show up in her life as you lift your eyes and beseech Holy Spirit God to touch and restore in the name of Jesus. This mom leaves the prayer center understanding that Jesus stepped in, the fever is gone, and her baby is well. Or, a broken-hearted dad who cannot provide for his family comes in and is looking for a job. While in the prayer center his cell phone rings with a job offer, or another guest waiting for prayer overhears his need and gives him a lead that becomes the answer to that prayer. Or the older gentleman who cannot have knee replacement surgery and desperately limps in on his cane—and leaves without needing it. The list continues.

Watching God show up in the lives of our neighbors is beautiful! One day an elderly gentleman, Ray, came to WLFJ for the first time. He looked down as he entered, obviously embarrassed to be there. He asked if we had a stove. A volunteer directed him to the prayer center where the inventory for furniture and appliances is kept. The person serving in the prayer center that day asked if she could pray for God to provide him with a stove. He was proud and said he had never asked anyone for anything in his entire life, but his stove was old and had simply quit working. He was too proud to tell his friends that his stove was broken because he didn't want anyone to know he couldn't afford another one. Ray agreed for the volunteer to pray so she asked the Lord to provide for His need and to please do it in such a way that he'd know that God had provided. She then checked our inventory and there was no stove. He was disappointed, but she told him to keep his eyes open to see how God might answer this prayer. She invited him to come back again to shop and to also stop for prayer. We agreed to continue praying with him until we saw GOD meet this need in his life. We are committed to never have our neighbors look to us for their answer, we want their focus on Jesus. We try to always direct their attention to Jesus as their provider.

The next morning was Thursday. We are not open to the public on Thursdays at the Raleigh facility. I saw a pickup truck pull into the loading dock early that morning and an older man jumped out and ran up the steps smiling. I realized this was the man who had needed a stove. He looked younger, more energetic, and much happier than when he had left the building the previous day. This was Ray's story: He arrived home to hear his phone ringing. When he answered it, his friend calling was angry and upset. He began to tell Ray how his daughter makes him so angry because she felt like nothing he had was good enough and how she was always bringing him things that he didn't want. On this day, he felt she had really stepped out of line. She had brought him a brand new stove and he hated it! His current stove was fine and he liked it! He asked Ray to please bring his pickup truck and help him take that new stove somewhere and give it away because it was in his way. Ray humbled himself and explained his situation to his friend. They took Ray's old stove to the landfill and moved the new stove into his house. I hugged Ray and said, "See how much God loves you. He wanted you to have a brand new stove. If you had received one from us, it would have been used." Ray left beaming. Jesus had shown up in his place of need.

On another day, Amy came to shop. She stopped in the prayer center and asked the volunteer for a mattress. Her son had serious back problems and was currently sleeping on the floor. The volunteer prayed for God to provide for this need. She checked our inventory, but we did not have a bed. Again the volunteer encouraged her to watch to see how God might provide and to keep coming back until this need was met. As Amy left our building, overcome with discouragement, she passed a large hotel. She noticed on their loading dock a tall stack of mattresses. She pulled into the hotel parking lot, went inside, and asked for the manager. She explained to him that she at was at WLFJ and a volunteer had prayed for her son to receive a mattress. She asked him if he could help her. He loaded up one of those brand new mattresses onto the top of her car. We all understood that God had stepped into her life in a personal way. We give away used, but good, mattresses all the time. This young boy needed a new one for his serious back issues.

Many times our volunteer, Margaret, or her team of prayer warriors, minister to someone in the prayer center, and a week later may minister to the same person again, and so on for several weeks before there is a breakthrough or until healing takes place. We always seek God's healing, however, every situation has a root cause. Often God wants to do the greater thing, which is to deal with the root. In the process, healing can also take place. Some things take time. God is both healer and freedom-giving God. There are those things which we do not understand. Margaret has been used by God many times as His tool in healing someone from sickness or releasing someone from a place of bondage. When her own precious daughter was battling cancer, Margaret stood by her bed as she slipped into her heavenly home, helpless to do anything. I remember hearing a pastor talk about the vast numbers that he has been allowed to pray for that have been healed as he stood helplessly by his dad's bed and could do nothing. The same disease which took his dad, he had seen disappear as he prayed for others. Sometimes in these very hard places, we see God show up and do a mighty work. Our community has been encouraged by Margaret's steadfast love for God and her faithfulness to pray for others even as she faced one of the greatest heartbreaks in her own life. It speaks volume to a hurting community to see those serving with difficult situations in their own lives, and yet not giving up on God. Those who serve at WLFJ are not without their places of hardship or even bondages. Many have financial hardships or relationship problems in their families or sickness and pain to handle. Servants of God are not exempt from problems, but they are carried and sustained by the loving One who has called them to serve in His Kingdom work!

With countless needs in the community, God is constantly revealing to us His Kingdom work in the midst of busy days. A regular guest, who we had often prayed with over the evil in her neighborhood, stopped to receive prayer. Through tears she shared that her son had been killed that week. She was coming to ask for prayer for her family as they worked through their deep pain and grief. The volunteer ministered to her and the presence of the Lord was amazing. Jesus touched her. She experienced His peace, presence, and comfort. The volunteer encouraged her to let go of the pain instead of trying to make sense of it, to leave it with Jesus to handle. She did! God had worked a miracle. Yet, there was another miracle about to happen. The man waiting after her to receive prayer (also a believer) told the volunteer that he wanted to forget all the things he had come in to receive. All he wanted now was to receive the kind of prayer ministry that this lady had experienced. God was calling him to surrender. They prayed and God challenged him to go to the neighborhood where this young man was killed to witness and minister to those caught in the enemy's evil trap. He accepted the challenge. What a humbling experience it was to witness the powerful moving of the Spirit in the lives of these two hurting people. Looking around at the circumstances of the day, it was a hot, sweaty, and busy day. If you looked with spiritual eyes, you could see the redeeming work of God taking what was a senseless death and turning it around for Kingdom purposes.

God often reminds us of one of the principles He taught us in the home ministry. We give our time and ourselves to Him. He is the one who works in the lives of our neighbors. When we are involved in the busy daily outreach at WLFJ, this is a good perspective to have. We are here to partner with God and if lives are changed, it is because they have responded to His work in their lives. It's God's ministry and God's results. I am called to be faithful, obedient, and to honor Him. This is great protection over us from the Lord. We do not carry the burden nor do we take credit for what only He can do. It is more important to do things God's way and to leave the outcome in His capable hands. *The horse is made ready for the day of battle, but victory rests with the Lord* (Proverbs 21:31, NIV).

It was one of those unusual days at WLFJ when we didn't have volunteer coverage and were not able to serve guests. We stayed on the sidewalk to see if we could minister to folks through prayer or simply listening. Wilbur lingered on the sidewalk and asked if we could pray with him. He did not give us his list of needs. Instead, he thanked God for what he had already received. He moved into an apartment of his own and was no longer living on the streets. He recently received Christ and was delivered from alcoholism. He did not talk about things such as no bed to sleep on or riding the bus to get here to be turned away. He asked for and received prayer and left smiling. The next day, we were open for guests and he returned to the ministry to shop. Wilbur stopped in the prayer center to receive prayer again. He left the building that day riding in a pickup truck driven by a volunteer with a mattress, boxed springs, television, microwave, linens, dishes, food, and a new fan loaded in the back. He was receiving more than a double portion. He was blessed for his willingness to embrace God's timing and plan. God gave us the standard that we are not to herd people into the building only to meet physical needs. If we cannot offer ministry, we do not open. Because our vision is to be a platform to display the unity of the Body of Christ, God has helped us to understand that we have to take care of the Body first, before the community. When we are short-handed of volunteers, we have to figure out what we can do well and then do it. We do not max out our brothers and sisters in Christ by trying to do more than God has equipped us to do on that day. It's easy to be tempted to think we can't turn someone away. However, WLFJ is never to be someone's answer. God might use us to help our community, but we want our community to depend on Jesus and not us.

There is much for all of us to learn as we wait on the Lord and follow His principles and instructions. Much more is happening in a day than we can see with our physical eyes. Walking in close tandem with Him is always the solution in every situation. This lovely ministry to Wilbur was a beautiful example of the blessings that follow when we do things God's way and in His timing.

As in years past, when someone living with us would need correction for not honoring the standards of our home, I am sometimes placed in a similar difficult situation at WLFJ when an honored guest behaves badly. A guest will sometimes disrespect a volunteer or the ministry in some way. They might steal or try to intimidate a leader, and we are obligated to speak correction into their lives. If they do not heed that correction, I have to tell them that their shopping privileges are suspended until they have a private meeting with me at another time. I hate when these things happen. However, I understand that this is really God's grace and His mercy poured into their lives. Many of those we serve have never had healthy confrontation for their behavior. People have either been intimidated by them and have given them their way, or have responded to them in anger. Neither is right. Nearly every time a situation such as this happens, if the person agrees to meet with me one-on-one one, God does a work in them before they arrive. Our time together will often become a stepping stone in their lives for good. God steps into these places and gives me an amazing ministry opportunity that might never have happened without the confrontation to their misbehavior. We are too quick to give up on each other. God is long suffering with us. This doesn't mean He ignores our sin, but He has factored it in already and taken care of it with the blood of Jesus. It frees us up to focus on our relationship with Him. One of our values at WLFJ is respect. We are called by God to respect each other and those we serve. Sometimes respecting someone is not allowing them to continue on the path they are walking without at least confronting it.

More than once I've had a child tell me that they were eighteen (which would allow them the opportunity to be a shopper) when I knew they were not. Usually they will come around and tell the truth. Many times their eyes are looking at their parent helplessly because the lie was the parent's idea. I always hug the child and thank them for being truthful. I send the child away to do something and then confront the parent.

"One day your child is going to lie to you," I'll say. "You'll ask them 'what makes you think it's all right to lie to me' and then you'll remember today and know that you taught them to lie."

Often I witness a parent asking their child's forgiveness and again recognize God has worked through correction. Helping people respect themselves also helps them respect others.

I was in the parking lot helping to bring folks in to shop when Tommy, who weeks earlier had been required to leave because of his very bad behavior, came up to me. I told him he needed to leave until he called me to make an appointment for us to talk together. (This is what I told him when I made him leave earlier.) He talked with me a bit and was obviously drinking. I asked him to leave. He started crying and asked if he was going to hell.

I said, "Hell is not somewhere that God sends us, it's a choice we make."

He began to sob. He shared that he had been diagnosed with AIDS and was dying. He asked again if he was going to hell. I invited him to come into the building if he would control himself. I was concerned because of the alcohol influence that he might not be able to behave. He told me he had been drinking, but he agreed to sit quietly. He said he knew he needed to quit drinking, but it was his only way of trying to escape his fear of dying. After hearing the brief message, I took Tommy to the prayer center. Don, one of our seasoned volunteers and a retired missionary, spent time with him and shared the good news of the gospel. Tommy made the choice of life and not death. He chose heaven and not hell. He chose Jesus! We could only praise the Lord for the beautiful way God stepped into a place of discipline and turned it into a place of salvation. A couple of weeks later, I was making announcements to the first group of the day.

As I looked up, there he sat, smiling, calm, and with a peaceful countenance. God had again done an amazing work.

One day an honored guest came to our door and said she only wanted to know how to say "thank you" to God. She did not ask to shop. A volunteer inquired what it was she wanted to thank God for. She began to weep. On a previous visit to the ministry, she had been heartbroken by the diagnosis she'd recently received from her doctor. He said she had incurable cancer over much of her body. She had received prayer and now there was no cancer to be found. She was as much in shock from God's miracle working in her life as she had been from the fatal diagnosis.

One of my favorite honored guests is Ms. Mattie. When she first came to WLFJ, she was a mixture of delight and exasperation. She is an elderly lady with a short fuse. Nearly every time she came, someone had to address her unkind words to other guests. One day I took her aside and asked her if she knew Jesus as her Savior. She wanted to know why I was asking her that question. I told her that she did not behave like someone who knew Jesus. Her response surprised me.

She said, "Well, help me be sure."

We talked a few minutes as I went over the gospel truths with her. We bowed our heads, and she prayed. Whether she had ever done this before or not, I wasn't sure. However, from that day forward we saw a difference in her. She sometimes lost her temper or was unkind, but even when it did happen, she was quick to repent and would try to make things right. I loved watching the change, but was also delighted to have her shop. One day she came to me with a special request. Her son needed community service hours for a traffic offense and she asked if he could earn them with us. We allowed him to come, and for the most part, he did a good job. One day, he came to the building to shop (on a different day from when he served as our volunteers are not allowed to shop and serve on the same day). He gave the volunteers a difficult time. He wanted special privileges because he was a volunteer. We quickly dealt with the issue, and as a result, his shopping and serving privileges were taken away. I told him to give me a call if he wanted his shopping privileges returned, however, his opportunity to volunteer could not be restored. He never called. One day Ms. Mattie came to me and said her son was prideful and would not call me, but he really needed to shop so she and I prayed for him. I was touched by her humility in seeking on his behalf and I encouraged her to have him call me, but he still did not call. Finally, one day, I told her to tell him to come back with her, talk to me for a few minutes, and I would allow him to shop. He came, but immediately tried to defend his bad behavior. I cautioned him to be quiet.

I said to him, "I have a place in heaven because of Jesus. You have a place here to shop because of your mother. The difference is that Jesus will never take heaven away. If you blow this chance here, it will never be given back to you."

He recognized this was not a place I was willing to compromise and didn't say a word. He has never caused a problem again, but has never been allowed to serve as a volunteer. It was important to me to bless Ms. Mattie and her sweet, loving heart. Ministry is not always pleasant, but it is all part of His work in our community and within us. I am sure Jesus did not enjoy turning over the tables in the temple or speaking corrections, but it was part of the work He was called to do.

God will never let us be someone's answer. He is their answer. He might allow us to be part of how He will help or work in someone's life. Chrissie was an honored guest who came to know Jesus in the prayer center at WLFJ. Much like Helen, who came years earlier to live with our family from the prison, Chrissie was not easy. She wanted to do right, but she often didn't. We would see her make some steps in her walk with the Lord, only to take another one backwards. She never became part of a local church family. We tell those who get saved at WLFJ that we are not their church, they need to find a church. We keep a list in the prayer center of churches by zip code. When someone comes to know the Lord, we try to give them a couple of churches in their area to help them begin their search for a church family. Some have been hurt by a church in the past and won't allow themselves to become part of a church body. When that happens, they usually don't grow. Like babies, new Christians need a family in order to grow. Chrissie would come to shop and often her mouth would get her in big trouble. There was a time when I had to take away her shopping privileges because she had behaved rudely. Later, she met with me, we prayed together and her privileges were restored. Sometimes she came in unkept in her appearance, wearing something inappropriate. More than once we gave her something different to wear or shared a nice Jesus t-shirt with her, telling her to throw away the one she was wearing when she got home. She had lived as part of the world for a long time and did not always understand what was decent and acceptable dress for a believer. Jesus' beautiful leadership team at WLFJ continued to work and work and work with Chrissie. She was still not going to church so we kept encouraging her to find a church family, but she never followed through. She needed the Body, and we couldn't give up on her. We saw the backwards steps happening less often as she made small but steady steps onward. One Saturday morning she came to shop. The next day, she took some of the food she had received to her mom for their Sunday lunch. As she sat in her mom's living room, she suddenly died of a heart attack. There are no words to express our gratitude to the Lord for allowing us to be in Chrissie's life. At times it was extremely hard, but she was worth it. To be a tool in the hand of our mighty God is an amazing privilege. He is the answer. We often are allowed to be the arrows pointing people to the Answer! We speak often of her and how we will enjoy spending eternity with a free and joyful Chrissie.

Miracles are instant, but healings are sometimes a process. There was a day that I knew I had pushed myself way too hard. I can get caught up in the whirlwind of a building that needs to be pulled into order, and before I know it, the building is in order and I am wiped out. This was the case one Monday evening. I came home knowing I had stepped over the line, and I was the one in the wrong! I took medication and went to bed. The next day I could still feel that place in my lower body that told me I'd messed something up. I suspected it was the bladder, but hadn't been to the doctor. What I knew was that something was not where it should be. It was my day off from the ministry and I had borrowed a DVD from the WLFJ library which caught my eye. It was a recorded worship time from years earlier and I was interested in watching it. As the recording began, I was drawn in and began to worship the Lord. They transitioned to a time of praying for people to be healed. I touched this lower area of my body and confessed to the Lord my bad stewardship over His body. I welcomed Holy Spirit God into my room and my body as I worshipped. The pain was gone, and whatever was out of place was now in place. I experienced the miracle of God in my body as I worshipped before Him with a worship team that had recorded this many years earlier. God's ways are often beyond our ability to understand.

Chapter 12
Forgiveness

You have made a wide path for my feet to keep them from slipping.
Psalm 18:36, NLT

For years, before God pulled back the curtain and allowed me to see the abuse in my life, I was often debilitated by migraine headaches which came on suddenly. I'd have the taste of metal in my mouth and a gradual but steady pressure which moved up the left side of my face and neck. For years, I took medication, rested, used ice packs, and tried to make it go away when I felt those first symptoms begin. Nothing touched it. After realizing that nothing I did made a difference, I got busy the moment I had that taste in my mouth and started pulling my household together, getting food ready for my family, and preparing the children for the next three days. Once it hit full force, I went into a dark room, placed ice packs on the left side of my face, propped up in bed, and endured the pain until it was over. Usually mid-way through the second day, I began to feel relief, and by the third day I could function again.

God healed me of those migraines but it was a process. That

process began when I learned about an important tool that God has given us. That tool is forgiveness. I thought I already knew about forgiveness. If someone hurt or offended me, I forgave them. However, I came to understand that forgiving and forgiving from the heart were two different things. I learned to visit that emotional place in order get to the root of how that offense made me feel. Once the Lord helped me diagnose how something made me feel, I could better and more completely forgive. If I felt rejection or neglect or condemnation, I would take forgiveness to that level. Learning to forgive also meant that I had to learn to forgive myself. Life was full of my own failures. We all have to deal with our foolish, careless, or deliberate sins and mistakes. To be able to bring them to God and have Him not only forgive, but also redeem them, means that we have to learn to forgive ourselves as well. He had me on a training ground for myself, but also so I would be able to pass it on to others. Learning to forgive God was the biggest hurdle for me.

Some of the greatest work God has done in me personally has been the result of learning to walk out forgiveness with others, myself, and even with God. My life has been forever changed by this simple but very powerful tool from God. In the early days of dealing with the abuse of my childhood, I took Leah and we went to the beach for a few days. I prepared a place for her to do her school work on the gazebo overlooking the ocean. She worked on school work while I walked down to the edge of the water, pacing back and forth keeping her in sight. I talked with God about what He had revealed to me earlier. There were two men in my childhood who I needed to forgive. I also needed to forgive my parents for allowing these men in my life. The place I could not seem to move past was that God—sovereign, loving, caring, compassionate, protector—could have stood by and allowed this to happen to a little girl. He put me in this family. He knew I would one day be in His family. He created me. He said He loved me, but I felt abandoned, unprotected, unloved, and extremely angry with Him. I walked the beach, kicking the water and screaming into the surf at God. Leah was working away on the gazebo while I was screaming at God.

In the same way that a child might need to forgive her parent because she couldn't understand why something was handled in a certain way, I knew I needed to forgive God. He was not wrong. He is perfect, holy, righteous, amazing God. He could do no wrong, but I couldn't enter in to an understanding of His ways in regard to this situation. I kicked the water.

God said to me, "Linda, you either side with me or you side with the enemy."

My response was out of my deep pain, and God knew it. "God, I do not want to side with either."

I understood God was saying to me that if I did not side with Him—accept His sovereignty and love—I would be siding with the enemy. Finally, in exhaustion, I said, "God, I side with you."

I began that day learning how to forgive from the heart, and that would become a powerful tool in my life. God spoke to me from His Word. *The secret things belong to the Lord our God, but the things revealed belong to us and to our children forever, that we may follow all the words of the law* (Deuteronomy 29:29, NIV). It made sense to me as a parent that there were some "secret things" that I chose not to share with my children, because they were not ready to understand. There may be a later time when I would "reveal" more information to them, but they would need to trust me until then. As a result of entering into this new place with God, I was totally healed from the migraine headaches. The deep pain in my life which had erupted through these monster head-aches had been diffused by a mighty God using His powerful weapon of forgiveness. God gives us many directions and commandments in His Word. He gives them to us for our good. Of course, as we walk out these places honoring Him, it brings Him glory. But, He also wants us to be blessed and protected. These directives are for our good. He wants our trust and we get to reveal our trust in Him with our obedience. The result is that we reap many blessings. We cannot lose when we obey Him.

God also used this experience to make changes to my parenting. God is the perfect parent. He lovingly and patiently allowed me to vent my emotions and to cry out to Him. He even allowed me to criticize Him. He's holy and righteous. There is no wrong in Him, yet He allowed me to say what I needed to say, to get it out, and to be ready to move on in my relationship with Him. There would be many times after this that I would say to my daughters, "You can say anything you need to say to me. I can handle your anger and disappointment with me." Once they would vent, I might ask them to go to their room to give their emotions an opportunity to calm down. Then we could talk again. God made Himself into a safe place for me, and I wanted to learn to be a safe place for my children and those entrusted into my care. In order to do this, I had to learn to rest in my position in Christ and not let their venting define me. It became a great relationship building tool for me. God wastes nothing!

Another component that God taught me as I walked this forgiveness road was to be aware of what I was thinking. I had to be quick not to accept every thought as generated by me. For instance, if I found myself thinking negative thoughts about another believer, I had to recognize that I was under attack by the enemy. I would quickly need to say, "This is not my thought." I had to move quickly not to take ownership of the thought. Yes, taking the thought captive was important. The way to do that was to understand this was not mine! God's Word declares that I am holy, set apart by God, a saint, and a co-worker with God. Negative, critical thoughts are the enemy's tool. The quicker I could recognize what was happening and take authority over it, by first declaring it was not my thought, and second, by replacing the thought with something else, the sooner it came to an end. I would immediately say aloud something positive and true about the person served up in the negative thought. I would declare their position in Christ and pray for God's blessing over them. These assaults quickly stopped because I took the enemy's trick and turned it against him instead of allowing him to control me. He would then flee. Once I forgave someone, if I continued to struggle with the offense, I reminded myself that this was already forgiven and began to pray for them. God was also teaching me to look for something positive to do. Even something small, like choosing to smile at a stranger, or leaving a candy bar on someone's desk could become a useful tool to diffuse the enemy. If his attacks generated positive and good, he would flee. This is warfare that is often missed and, if overlooked, can cause us to stay in a place of defeat. God has made us to be victorious.

God was also teaching me to dig deeper to be thorough with forgiveness. There was a sister in Christ who was in my life frequently. I loved her and enjoyed her, yet when I was with her, I would often feel anger rising up in me. I had to be on my guard all the time when I was with her to keep from being offended and defensive around her. I forgave her for everything I could possibly think of and yet received no permanent relief. I asked the Lord to help me understand what was going on and how to deal with it. One night, I woke from sleep with a start and my mind went back to a place in my childhood. God began to replay event after event in my life when one particular adult in my childhood consistently ridiculed me, spoke harshly to me, and negatively compared me to her child. As I lay in bed pondering this little slideshow, I began to realize that my sister in Christ had the same build, hair color, some of the same mannerisms, and was about the same age as the lady in my childhood at the time she hurt me. God had revealed the problem. I slipped out of bed and went to the living room. For some time, I sat there listing everything I had seen in my memory and other things God brought to my mind. I carefully forgave the person from my childhood and asked the Lord to heal my damaged emotions. Immediately, I saw relief from these symptoms when I was with my sister in Christ. Because I had built a habit of being apprehensive when around her, it took a while for that habit to subside. I learned from this experience to examine a situation more carefully when forgiveness did not bring the results I knew it should. God is a wonderful counselor and teacher. When we cry to Him for answers, He is quick to respond. He is a great communicator.

I also learned that forgiveness could be on several different levels. For instance, when I forgave the men from my childhood, it needed to touch all the areas of my life that had been affected by them. I had to forgive how the abuse had affected my parenting, my marriage, my identity, and my view of myself. Sometimes, I needed to walk it out for a few days before I could move on to the next area. Forgiveness and healing go hand in hand. As I chose to forgive, I also asked the Lord to heal. A new place of healing often prepares the way for a new level of forgiveness.

These lessons would become invaluable to me in situations I faced over the years. When I faced the hurt with Mr. Clyde, or John, or the church, or unjust authority, I had learned that running quickly to God and working through forgiveness allowed me to function better in dealing with all my emotions, and enabled me to take the next step. I was then able to rest in His sovereignty and look forward with expectancy to the redemption of God. No one could mess up God's plan for my life. There was nothing that God could not redeem and use for good. One of my go-to places during this time was Isaiah 45:2-3: *I will go before you and will level the mountains; I will break down gates of bronze and cut through bars of iron. I will give you the treasures of darkness, riches stored in secret places, so that you may know that I am the Lord, the God of Israel, who summons you by name.* I would often say to the Lord, "I need to find the treasure you have for me in this dark place."

How does this amazing God of ours work? He is great beyond words. He takes those things done against us or our own failures that are given over to Him, and actually uses these painful places for great good. There are storehouses of treasures hidden away for us if we will only bring the hurt, shame, regret, or struggle to Him. He buys them back and they become Kingdom deposits. To share these incredible truths with someone who feels that their life is destroyed brings them great hope and becomes another way that God works to bless us.

There have been many treasures that God has given me. There is a place of sweet intimacy with Him that comes out of painful, restored places. There is also the amazing pleasure of being His instrument of blessing in the lives of others. Countless ladies in the prison Bible Study benefited from that day I spent with God kicking at the ocean and learning how to side with Him. The beautiful ladies over the years that have traveled through our home have learned the same principles from God that brings freedom and deliverance. Today, as a needy community comes to WLFJ, my eyes are searching for those that God would have me or another team member minister to with the truth of God's riches stored in the secret and hurting places of life. One of the things that we as a team desire for our community is for the day to come when our honored guests will thank God for their hard places because they became the entrance of God into their lives. We will all go through hard and painful places. This is part of life on planet earth. However, to go through difficult places alone, or not to see them redeemed and used for good is a terrible thing! God taught me that we have to be willing to push through with Him to get to the other side. It's well worth the investment.

Another benefit produced through forgiveness is seeing the beautiful unity of the Body of Christ displayed. When iron sharpens iron there are sometimes sparks. No one agrees with someone else all the time. At WLFJ we choose to focus on the one place that all believers can agree—there is only one way to the Father and that is through the precious blood of Jesus. Even as we choose this place of agreeing, there are times that we can rub each other wrong. There are times that we have to decide to go with being a team player instead of getting our way. We can easily be convinced that our opinion doesn't matter or that a comment made was meant to hurt us or communicate something negative about us. We have to guard ourselves and not allow anyone to take on the label of enemy. We all belong to Jesus. Our enemy is not flesh and blood, and certainly is not a brother or sister-in-Christ. There is no virtue in seeing sin in each other. The virtue is to see Jesus in our fellow believers. Walking out forgiveness daily makes a team strong and allows unity to be seen.

The vision of WLFJ is to be a platform to display the unity of the Body of Christ. We are one. Often we, the Body of Christ, do not act as one, but we are the amazing, beautiful, Family of God. We need places where we can step outside our local church and connect with other believers to allow our love for each other to be seen. Jesus said the world would know that we belong to Him by our love for each other. Any parent of two or more children can tell you that when brothers and sisters are getting along and showing love to each other, the parents also feel loved. Family is very important to God. It was His idea. We see family valued greatly in the Word of God. The local church family is a picture of the big Family of God. The Bible is full of instructions to parents on how to relate to each other and to their children. Each of us comes to the Family of God on the same footing. Jesus died for us so that we can be right with God and be part of His Family. For family to work correctly, we have to get along. God does not favor one child above another. All have their place, and all fit together to make up the whole. The Word tells us that how we treat each other is actually taken personally by Jesus. To love each other is to love Him. To hurt each other is also to hurt Him. We have to work at peace, it doesn't just happen. Jesus died so we could be in His Family. We have to die as well to make family work. We must prefer others more than ourselves, encourage each other, help each other, love, respect, honor, and the list goes on. Every person in the family is important, yet each person must make sacrifices for the greater good of all. It's not easy. It's hard work, and forgiveness is a major component.

Jesus teaches much about forgiveness. I am sure that at least one of the reasons He does is because we, as the Church, need to learn to walk it out with each other. It's easy to talk about forgiveness. It's quite another thing to truly forgive and walk it out. We have to get good at it. However, like everything else, the way you get good at something is to practice it a lot! I am very thankful for all those in the family of God (and especially my personal family) who have learned this well and walk in forgiveness toward me. We all come from different places, backgrounds, and influences as we walk planet earth together. We will not see eye to eye on many things, and God is at work in each of us differently, and often in very different places. We are God's little 'dust' people (Psalm103:14). He remembers and factors in our frailty. We'd do well to do the same toward our brothers and sisters in Christ. I often hear stories from our volunteers about how people are set free or healed because they learn to forgive those who have hurt them. A young man sat broken and angry as he recounted the terrible things done against him by his employer. He walked out of the prayer center with peace and a joyful countenance when he realized that forgiving the one who hurt him was actually his way of turning the situation over to God for Him to deal with. Vengeance belongs to God. When we learn to leave things with God and allow Him to work in the situation, we experience a release from the burden. We take back the control over our lives and our enemy no longer has power to use that person to control and hurt us. It's easy to get tripped up thinking we have the right to be angry or hurt. The truth is we have the right to be free. Jesus died so we could be free. We must choose to die to our perceived rights so that we can walk in the freedom that is ours in Christ Jesus our Lord! As we love each other, God's Word tells us that the world sees that we belong to Jesus. The display of unity is often the greatest miracle of all!

Chapter 13
Family is Worth the Effort

Lord, you have assigned my portion and my cup; you have made my
lot secure. The boundary lines have fallen for me in pleasant places;
surely I have a delightful inheritance.
Psalms 16:5-6, NIV

One of the things I had enjoyed when living in the farmhouse
was the circle driveway. We lived off a main thoroughfare and
the Body of Christ dropped by often for tea or fellowship. It was
busy, but a place where the Spirit of God was at work.

When we moved to our new place, we found it to be much
the same way. There was no longer the swing on the big front
porch, but there was the swing Greg built for Tara under the big
oak tree which we all enjoyed. The Body of Christ stopped by
frequently and Holy Spirit God was at work in this house, too.
With the constant influx of folks who lived with us, those who
stopped by for fellowship or ministry, and the parade of people
who came to receive food as God gave birth to WLFJ, we were a
busy household. I'm not a people person, but I loved the fellowship of the Body! I continue to long for a circle driveway in our

big front yard. It speaks many good things to me!

When the home ministry came to an end, we settled into the house as two families living together. Greg and Sam converted the laundry room into a small bedroom for my grandchildren, Isaac and Savannah, so that a crib and a youth bed fit perfectly. They built a new laundry room and bathroom where a closet inside the house backed up to a storage room in the garage. As the children grew, that old laundry room was turned into a two-story room for my grandson Aaron when Sam and Greg built a loft in the attic and added a ladder connecting the spaces.

When my dad went to be with the Lord in 2005, we used part of the inheritance I received to remodel the garage into a bedroom, bath, and sitting room for Sam and me. This freed up our old room for our granddaughters, Victoria and Caroline. Our granddaughter, Savannah, moved into the third bedroom, and grandson, Isaac, took up residence in the sunroom. We laughed about this house having elastic walls. It wasn't perfect, but it was God's provision for us. We learned more about deferring to each other in order to make this strange living situation work. We were able to live with less money coming in as we pooled our resources. For a short period of time, Leah and her husband, Michael, lived with us while they were in a place of transition. Our family was called to a different lifestyle. God was doing a work in us, and this was another time of preparation. We look back and see the dots connecting to WLFJ as the ministry has also become a family, a house where God shows up, a place of fellowship, and a place of love and acceptance in the Body of Christ. As that dock door rises each day in the Raleigh facility and activity begins, there is a greater thing that happens besides serving our neighbors. That thing is called family. We witness this in the growing Johnston County facility as well.

As time continued to pass, everyone was involved at WLFJ. Sam handled several store pickups, all the banking and post office runs, and was also involved in electrical wiring, building bathrooms, and repairing whatever was broken at the time. With a ministry housed in an old warehouse building, there were many opportunities for Sam's abilities to be used. Leah's husband, Michael, jumped in to help with pickups scheduled around his full-time job. As their boys, Grayson and Sammy, were born, Leah transitioned from supervising Saturday volunteers to bookkeeping and leading our administrative team. She now helps with pickups and is also serving as leader of the Sunday team in our new outreach in Johnston County. Tara was the main connection to the home ministry and I was full-time at WLFJ. As the home ministry phase came to an end, life was still busy on the home front for Tara with five children. She currently heads up our amazing prayer team and is able to schedule our trucks for pickups from home.

Greg served part-time at WLFJ as he, for a time, was also the pastor of our church. He is now full-time at WLFJ serving in the role of Director of Community Relationships. He works closely with all the other ministries, nonprofits, and merchants who partner with us. It is a great blessing for us to work with others who are also serving our community.

Once at Christmas, another ministry came to us for help. They had expected toys to arrive on a particular day, but the toys did not arrive. With people coming to be served and no toys to give away, they were in a hard place. God blessed us that year with so many toys that we were able to generously share. Every day other partners come to our loading dock to share their extras with us. If we are running short on something, we have people we can call for help. It works both ways! Most of these relationships are in the Body of Christ. It's another way that together we can shine Jesus and be used to make a difference in our community. We love being team players. We value that God has entrusted us with a piece in His big puzzle of building His Kingdom on earth as it is in Heaven. We purpose to steward our piece well and are blessed to also connect our piece with others. The Body of Christ is wonderful.

It's easy to see that our household is busy and different from most. As time has passed, there have been constant changes, adjustments, and needs to cover. We have often wondered why God called us to live this way. He has all the resources in the world and could have easily provided for us to live separately.

Leah and Michael's family currently lives five minutes away. We are together all of the time as we serve together. God has done and continues to do a work in us, which seems always to be a time of preparation. We are three very distinct and different families that together make up another big family. It's much like the great Body of Christ. We are all individuals and families, living different and often complicated lives, but we are One. We are the Body of Christ.

In this odd family of ours, we've had many individual needs. God has worked in our lives in different ways. We have each had our things to work through. As we continue to live life on planet earth with the same needs that all other individuals and families have, there have been times when we have misunderstood each other or been misunderstood. We have each needed space of our own at times. Our individual families have sometimes needed to pull aside and make that family the priority of the moment. Writing about it can make it sound like constant fun and games, and it has been wonderful and amazing, but it has also been difficult and stretching at times. We each have said things we should not have said, and acted in ways that were wrong. We've learned that it is God's house and we cannot have an "ours or theirs" mentality. It is His! We have not always had the luxury of setting up things to our individual preferences. But, we have learned that everyone's needs are important and everyone's desires should be considered. By the grace of God, it has worked! We are blessed.

I sometimes tell people that we are the best forgivers in the world. We have learned that living together in harmony means that we have to forgive each other. Iron sharpens iron; that is true. It is also true that in the sharpening process there are also some pokes and injuries. God has made provision for this and part of that provision is again His tool called forgiveness.

This is what we've learned: we will forgive. We will work at these relationships. We will. We will. We will. This family is too important not to keep working at it. We value our relationships in this odd but wonderful family more than we value getting our own way, or having the last word, or harboring an attitude.

Sometimes others have to carry me and sometimes I have to carry them, but it is worth the work. It is worth the time investment because everyone in this family is important. No one will be left out regardless of a bad attitude or place of struggle. As time has passed, children have gotten older, needs have changed, we've all had to transition and be flexible. We value this family that God has put together. We love this amazing God that has given us this privilege. We will honor Him!

Over the years many people have come to me and made statements like, "It's good God didn't call my family to live together like this," or "Your family is very different from mine." In reality, our family is made of the same human fabric as everyone's family. We are hard to live with at times and struggle, too. It is true that God called us to live like this and most are not. However, the same principles that God has taught us apply to everyone to one degree or another. In every relationship we have to decide if the relationship is worth more than being regarded as right. Is it worth the effort to keep working at it until it is good? Forgiveness is important in every family. We have to make the plan ahead of time to stick with it and not give up. Families are worth the investment—human families and the Family of God. There are situations which require us to set aside time to spend with the Lord until we get His perspective. We don't know how to respond to people without His wisdom. This sharpening process which we go through with other humans is worth the effort. In our family, we can't afford to let walls build up. I talk to folks that have not talked to some of their family members in weeks, months, even years. This does not honor the Lord, and it also affects our walk with the Lord. This is huge.

If we have a chronic problem dealing with a specific person, God is at work in this situation. There is something He wants us to learn. There is something deeper than the surface problem which we need to dig through to get to the good that God has for us. These situations can be some of the greatest tools that God uses to reveal things to us about ourselves which we might not learn otherwise. We do not ever want to put ourselves in the position of forcing another person to choose between us and someone else. That is not God's way. Learning how to live to-gether as children of the King of Glory, enjoying what He has provided for each of us, and bringing glory to our heavenly Fa-ther in our love for each other is worth all the effort. We are blessed, but even more important, we bless our great God!

There are many threads that run through this book—family, ministry, God's faithfulness, redemption—and one of those threads is forgiveness. God continually reveals over and again the impossibility of walking in tandem with Him without the constant use of His forgiveness tool! We need to learn it, and then learn it again on another level. It's fundamental to enjoying freedom and victory in Christ Jesus. The Lord reminds us not to allow the sun to go down on our anger. He also instructs us in 2 Corinthians 2:11 that to fail to forgive opens up a door allowing our enemy to outwit and control us. We have to be smart in the Lord and in His ways of freedom. When we harbor bitterness and anger, and refuse to forgive someone who has hurt us, we actually open ourselves up for the enemy to work in our lives. We open a door that connects us to the things in the other person that the adversary controls. We can easily take God's warnings lightly, but bitterness and a failure to walk out forgiveness are expensive.

Once we have taken something to the Lord and He has for-given us, He doesn't hold it against us. Sometimes we misunder-stand and think it means God never brings it up to us again. There is sometimes great value in spending time with the Lord with the desire to understand how a thing happened and how to benefit from the experience in the future. This also applies in our relationship with others. When I've forgiven someone, I do not need to run to them and tell them I've forgiven them. That is between me and the Lord. However, once forgiveness is handled and I've had time for my emotions to calm, there could be bene-fit in talking it through. It is important to seek the Lord to under-stand my motivation before I try to talk with someone. But, there are times, for the sake of the relationship, when it is good to dis-cuss it with the person. Sam and I might have something come up in our relationship which I feel the need to bring to the Lord and choose to forgive Sam. Once it is all settled and I have no motivation to try to get back at him or to make him pay, it can be healthy for our relationship for me to go to him and discuss it. I know he loves me and he did not want me hurt. He might have said or done something innocently, but I took it wrong. Either way, our relationship is strengthened when we can discuss it and learn from it. Only the Lord can show us when this is an action we need to take. Many relationships can benefit from this further step. Relationships take hard work! They do not get good or stay good without a time investment. If we are not working on them regularly, we are losing ground. It is easy for misunderstandings and the busyness of life to take a toll on them.

One of my favorite accounts in the Bible is Mary, Martha, and Lazarus. They were a bit of an odd family, too. They loved Jesus and He was always welcomed in their home. I love to imagine Jesus and the disciples showing up at their home, staying a few days, eating together, and enjoying the fellowship of this family. I'm quite sure that their house, too, had elastic walls as they made room for all that traveled with Jesus, as well as those who came to the door to see Him. They found themselves in the midst of a difficult and painful place as Lazarus was sick and dying. They called for Jesus to come, but He did not come, He waited while Mary and Martha watched Lazarus die. I'm sure they had to deal with some forgiveness as they walked this road. They had seen Jesus heal many people, and they had always made a place for Jesus to be in their home. Now in their place of need, it must have seemed to them that Jesus had disregarded their cry for help. Yet, nothing was further from the truth. Jesus loved them greatly, and out of this place of intimacy and relationship with this family, He trusted them to be good stewards of this hard place. This was a stewardship; It was not a place of being neglected. Jesus trusted them to not understand. He trusted them to go through a painful place of feeling neglected and misunderstood. He trusted them because He was going to use their relationship to make Himself known to an on-looking world. I have documented often in old journals times when I've ask the Lord why we have been called to this lifestyle. Sometimes I've even dared to tell Him it's too hard or too much. Yet, He lovingly reminds me that this is a privilege, an entrustment, a stewardship, and the blessings are much greater than the momentary cost.

Mary and Martha witnessed the most amazing miracle. They stood by the grave of their precious brother who had been dead for days. They watched Jesus weep with them, only to hear Him a few minutes later cry out for Lazarus to come out. He did! We see Mary, Martha, and Lazarus again after Lazarus' resurrection enjoying a meal together, enjoying fellowship with Jesus, and worshipping Him from a deeper place of intimacy because He had trusted them with this difficult place. They would say it was worth it. They would say they were the most blessed of all. They were privileged to be an instrument in the hand of God to bless others and to reveal Jesus as the Resurrection and the Life.

One morning, as I sat pondering before the Lord and enjoying His presence, He gave me understanding that was a new revelation. Sometimes I can sense there is something I need to understand, but cannot seem to wrap my mind around it. Jesus is good to keep working with me and not letting me miss anything He wants me to grasp. He has given WLFJ the vision to be a platform to display the unity of the Body of Christ. It is not an easy vision, because we, His Body, are not easy! Unity is not about agreeing on all doctrine. Unity is about fighting together as a family instead of fighting against each other. Unity means standing together for the greater good of the whole! He revealed to me that our family has been given a stewardship from Him for the greater Body of Christ. If we are going to call the Family of God to come together and serve and bring glory and honor to Him, we have to first live it ourselves. In the same way that our family is worth the effort, His Family is worth the effort. If we were not called to a daily refresher course in family and living in unity, we could very easily forget and lose focus on what He has called us to walk at WLFJ. I have to love His Family even more than I love my family. I have to be long suffering and patient, forgiving, and accepting of His Family, just as He has called me to be with my family. WLFJ is not our family's ministry. It is His

Family's Ministry! Our family is one part of His Family. Like all other families we are precious to Him, and we carry a piece in His plan. We need to steward our piece well.

The stewardship for us is to do well at home what He has called us to speak into the greater Body of Christ. Family has become a precious thing to us so that we are willing to work through the issues to get to the good place. It is a constant place of learning and growing, of accepting and understanding, and of trusting God that He is working it all out for good and for blessing! With so many different parts of the Body of Christ coming together to serve at WLFJ, it's very important that we value each other above having our own way. The Word says that the world knows we belong to Jesus by the love we have for each other. We want the world to look inside WLFJ and see our love for each other and know this is Jesus' place. We love up on Jesus, by loving up on each other. Jesus died for me, but He also died for my brother or sister in Christ. I'm loved no less or more than anyone else. These are important and hard truths and are worthy of the practice needed to get it right and to walk it well.

We have a volunteer orientation class which shares the principles that God has given to us and helps everyone be of the same mindset when we come to serve together. It's very easy to think this ministry is about serving the poor and seeing people saved. But, this ministry is all about Family. His Family comes together to show the world that we belong to Jesus by our love for each other. There are principles that God has given us to set us up to do just this. For instance, we only allow the number of people to come in and be served as we have volunteers to cover. We are about ministry. We are not about herding people through the doors to see how much stuff we can give away. The Body has been called to minister. If we are being overrun by the crowd, we can't minister. Sometimes that means that we might have to close down early to really minister to the community that is in the building and not max out our volunteers for that day. God would never have us overwork or take advantage of our volunteers simply to give someone a bag of food. We are here to shine Jesus and give Him away. We are going to take care of Family.

It's important to us that our community sees the Family of God blessing each other. Our prayer is that they will desire the same relationships for themselves.

In the days of the home ministry, God taught us that these precious honored guests in our home were in many ways treated like family but they were not actual family. If family was being challenged, we might need to plan a night when we'd ask someone to invite our honored guest to their home for dinner or out for an evening to give our family time alone. Between guests, we'd take some time off from ministry to just be family. If our guest made plans to visit their family or to be gone for a day or so, we would often take that as opportunity to focus on our family. If we don't take care of family, we can't help others effectively, and we set a poor example of the priority of family. Keeping our focus right so we honor what God has called us to do is very important.

We are open to the community four days each week in Raleigh, but we have two other days each week to stock shelves, clean up, have fun together as family, and have a break before bringing the community back in to receive. We try to take care of practical things first so we can look out for Family. In our early days, we were open 6 days a week, but this was too difficult to maintain. Less is often better than more when it's done well. Our values, respect, compassion, honor, integrity, and love, are important to extend to the community that we serve. These same values must be extended to each other, too.

When I first took over the role of director for the ministry, I felt overwhelmed with thinking how I could possibly lead this work. God took me to the account of Solomon in the Old Testament. God showed me that Solomon was given credit for many things including the job of building the temple, yet Solomon didn't build the temple. Solomon had wonderful teams which came together under his leadership and built the temple. God instructed me to build teams. That's my role. I build the teams because this ministry is not about one person leading; it's about a team of leaders pulling together to make it happen. We have a governing board that is a team, an advisory board that is a team, and a pickup team that goes to grocery stores, merchants, and homes to collect resources to give away. We also have an administrative team, and a prayer team. Together the work is done.

At WLFJ there is a wonderful leadership team that does exactly what the name says. They lead the ministry each day at WLFJ. It is a team of people, each with their own family unit, each with their own needs, and their different place of growth in their walk with the Lord. However, they come together and they are family as they serve together in His ministry. As a team they have learned to defer to each other, to love and care for each other, to protect each other, to pray for each other, and to stand as one. Often there are differences of opinion or perspective but each person is quick to share their position and then look for the place of unity. Unity doesn't mean agreeing. It means standing together as one for the greater good of the whole. These are the people that set this example with the volunteers who come in to serve. Family members don't take sides or gossip or pull against each other. Family is a covenant relationship with Jesus as the head and center. It is a wonderful blessing to work with this amazing team of leaders and be part of their WLFJ family. The benefits are great. This, too, is a stewardship from the Lord. I love seeing the huge diversity in the Body of Christ. Personalities are different, backgrounds are different, giftedness and talents are different, and yet when we embrace this diversity, we find completeness.

Watching all the pieces come together to make the whole is fun and a daily miracle. Larry, a ball coach and retired businessman, heads up our loading dock and is the principle person to sort all the donated clothing. In one week, we give away nearly 10,000 clothing items. All these donated clothes have to be sorted, hung, and moved to the public area before they are given away. This is a huge undertaking and it takes a lot of people to make it happen. Judy and Danette sort and assemble all the household items. It takes a team to make sets out of sheets and put together dishes, glasses, flatware, etc., from the many pieces that come in daily. Becky leads the volunteer orientation class and heads up our display of clothing in the public area. Jim organizes and prepares our daily plan for the non-perishable foods and the deli table. Lori, a mom of five and Spanish teacher, translates most of our handouts into Spanish and interprets most messages for our Spanish speaking guests. She sorts the hundreds of books given away each week, getting rid of anything inappropriate. Margaret heads up our prayer center volunteers. Charla, with Danette, provides a daily plan for breads and sweets. Catherine serves on the administrative team; Karn moves from place to place as a need arises; Ray oversees the produce area, and along with most of these other leaders, has a specific day to co-coordinate the outreach. All serve at least ten hours each week and several serve twenty or more hours weekly. They are leaders with abilities and giftedness who could all be doing something else. All are well-trained and cross-trained and often help to cover for each other. They choose to pour their lives into this Kingdom work. Their hearts and their treasures are in heaven.

As we have been building the new outreach in Johnston County, there have been plenty of times that the volunteers who showed up outnumbered those coming to receive. We have used this as a great opportunity to help our new volunteers understand what we are all about. If we learn to do family well, we will serve the community well. Often, we will tell the volunteer team that even if no one shows up to be served, we can fulfill our vision—to be a platform to display the unity of the Body of Christ. We can enjoy each other, fellowship together, stock shelves, hang clothes, and enjoy being family. Guests always come, but Family comes first!

We need each other. The Body of Christ is made up of many parts. Each part is very important because together we make up the whole. We learn from each other. We refine each other. We blend together our different gifts and abilities and make each other complete. No one is called to serve alone. We need accountability. We need encouragement. I'm thankful for a board of directors to answer to and be accountable to because this is a protection for me. God's called me to lead, but He has called me to have advisors and people along the way to help me lead. Together we are powerful. Together we stand strong.

Jesus was headed to the cross when He prayed to the Father that we (His Children) would be one as He and the Father are One. He prayed that we would be so totally One that it would declare that the Father sent the Son. This is huge! Our oneness displayed reveals that the Father sent the Son. Jesus was headed to the torment of the cross, and we were on His mind. Our oneness was that important to Him. If it's that important to Him, it has to be that intentional for us. It won't just happen. We have to do our part to make it happen. There is beautiful diversity and many differences in the Body of Christ. Our enemy has done a great job of getting us to believe that the differences and diversity mean that we have to separate from each other. God has called us to be part of a local church, but God has also called us to display that we are One with His amazing Body.

Displayed unity is important. The more we connect together, the brighter we can shine Jesus to an on-looking world and the more we can be salt in a world that is filled with corruption. America is in a place of great need. We have failed as Christ' Body to be salt and light. We have allowed ourselves to be corrupted instead of deterring corruption. We look around at all the political and legislative battles going on in our nation. Everyone has their own opinions and too often feel the need to express them. Yet, we find ourselves swatting at these issues instead of cleaning up our hearts to better honor our God. It is a bit like swatting at flies when we need to get rid of the garbage and then the flies will be gone. As the Body of Christ in America, we need to get the trash out of our hearts and join with our brothers and sisters in a unified way and watch as God gets rid of these annoying flies. There have to be places where we step outside the local church and join arms and shine Jesus. The more we stand together, the greater impact we will have on the world around us. We have to repent. We have to unite. We have to cry out together that the Lord will forgive us, revive us, be merciful and heal our land. We are the amazing, beautiful, holy, powerful, and loved children of the King of Glory. We have to pull together which is often difficult and hard work. This is our time. We need to be good stewards of it.

We have hurt each other, and we have been hurt. When I look at my own path, I see a pattern that the most hurtful places came from within the Body of Christ. Family hurts are deeper and greater than any other hurts. Love gives someone the ability to also hurt. We have to fight for and not against each other. The places that I have been hurt within the Body of Christ have become the greatest opportunities to forgive and love and fight harder for the Body of Christ. I have wrestled this out often before the Lord. There was that time when a brother in Christ said hurtful things to me about my children. As a mother, those things stabbed my heart deeply. I struggled to forgive him. I did not want anything to do with him. I cried in the presence of the Lord, trying to make sense of it. The Lord allowed me some time to work through it. He knew I was forgiving, but it was a process. Finally, one day in my place of struggle, God gently reminded me that He knew how I felt. Every time I have spoken a negative or critical word to someone about another believer, I have been guilty of stabbing the heart of God. These are His children. He takes it very personally when I have said hurtful things about His children, and yet, He has forgiven me. Yes, forgiven me, but also continued to love me, associate with me, desired to be part of my life, and continued to build intimacy with me. It cut me to the core to think that my friend's hurtful remarks to me were only dim examples of the great ways I have hurt the heart of my Heavenly Father. The church split that broke my heart, even more so, broke the heart of God. When I hurt a brother or sister in Christ, I hurt the heart of the Father. To forgive and love someone who has hurt us gives us the opportunity to look more like Jesus. He is the best forgiver of all.

Chapter 14
Walking Out Hope

*Know therefore that the Lord your God is God; he is the faithful
God, keeping his covenant of love to a thousand generations of those
who love him and keep his commands.*
Deuteronomy 7:9, NIV

When my grandson, Aaron, was born, I couldn't shake the above
verse from my mind and heart. I said to the Lord many times,
"One day Aaron's grandson's, grandson's, grandson will say 'we
are blessed because my great, great, great grand-mommy, Linda,
turned her heart to the Lord.'" I loved thinking that the decisions
I made in this life to seek the Lord would bless for generations to
come in my family. I wanted all generational bondage broken
and for those coming after me to walk in the fullness of all God
has accomplished for them.

I know beyond any doubt that my parents loved me and did
their best to provide for everything I needed. Because they were
raised out of the depression, meeting needs translated to them as
finances. They worked very hard to be sure that our family's
financial needs were met. My dad built a very good business to

support our family, and my mom was also successful in the business world. Both came from alcoholic fathers and their heritage was difficult. My dad's family knew much brokenness with a very large family that struggled to provide for needs, but was also riddled with generational sins. My mother's mother worked hard to keep her very large family afloat with a husband who had a promising career but wasted his money on alcohol. My mom and her siblings ranged from grabbing hold of the Lord and walking with Him, to following the footsteps of their dad. For some, it was a combination. There are aunts and uncles who God has used to bless, encourage, and pray for me. I am thankful for each one and the part they have played in my heritage.

One of those special family relationships was my mom's cousin. She lived with my mom's family while she was growing up so I always thought she was mom's sister. We called her Aunt Lib. She never married. She had brokenness, loss, and pain in her life, but she never allowed it to stop her and she served the Lord wherever she went. Aunt Lib blessed countless children as she served for many years in a summer camp that she helped to start. The blessings continued as she taught the Bible in public schools, and as she served on the mission field. She also blessed me although we didn't see her often. She was a busy, for the Lord, lady! When she came to visit us, it was an event. She loved my mom's good country cooking so Mom always prepared especially great meals when Aunt Lib came. Aunt Lib's visits changed our home for the days she was there. She valued children and brought that place of value with her when she came to our home. She listened to the children with true interest, and she treated us with love, respect, and compassion. I know that she also prayed for me and my family. When I came to know the Lord, I realized immediately that the thing I valued so much about Aunt Lib was Jesus. I couldn't wait to see her and share with her my new life in Christ. My children were blessed to have Aunt Lib in their lives as well. She lived to be over a hundred years old. In the weeks before her death, I was reading about the last days of Elijah's life. *When they had crossed, Elijah said to Elisha, 'Tell me, what can I do for you before I am taken from you?' 'Let me inherit a double portion of your spirit,'* Elisha replied (2Kings 2:9, NIV). For several days I found myself saying to the Lord, "I wish I had the nerve to ask for a double portion of Aunt Lib's spirit, but I would be forever blessed to have her same spirit." Sometimes in the night after that, I would say, "Double portion" over and again. Aunt Lib was God's tool in my life as she lived her life empowered by Holy Spirit God and not labeled by her past or her lack.

I never grow tired of watching God take hurt, pain, and brokenness and turn it into Kingdom gain and blessing. My dad and mom deposited good into my life. I remember as a child we lived across the street from the railroad tracks. Regularly, hobos would jump from the train cars to seek food. Many would find themselves at my mother's kitchen door. There was one house closer to the tracks than ours but I never saw anyone stop there. Looking back, I suspect we were marked in some way as a safe and good place to stop. Mom could always come up with food to fix a nice plate for someone. In my memory, I can still see a man sitting on our back stoop with a huge glass of iced tea and a plate brimming over with mother's food. She was a great cook and could make a yummy meal from anything. Often they left our porch with a paper bag in their hand with a sandwich or snack for down the road. We were never afraid of these travelers. Mother made us stay away from them, but not for our protection. It was to protect them from embarrassment. My little brother, Larry, was the one who always struck up conversations with these visitors. They always enjoyed him.

My mother was the life of any party. She was funny and people loved being around her. At her funeral, her friend, Nita, told stories of how she was loved and how funny she was and how she always reached out to others. She made any task fun and could stir up laughter from any gathering of people. There was great brokenness in her life, but in many ways, she didn't allow that brokenness to hurt others. It did eat away at her though. When I first became aware of my abuse, I went to her and tried to talk to her about it. I will always remember her response. She said, "That stuff happens to everybody." I was in shock. It does not happen to everyone. Her response confirmed what I knew. She, too, had experienced sexual abuse. I would have appreciated her being able to talk with me and share my grief over what had happened, but that was not the case. But, it helped me understand some of her choices and ways. She wanted everyone to think she was happy go lucky all the time, but in the last years of her life, she had to admit that she needed help. That was a difficult place for her. I love thinking of her walking those golden streets and enjoying her new life without the pain and brokenness that followed her most of her life on earth. She understands better than me today that brokenness does not disqualify us. Brokenness can be another opportunity used by God to display His greatness.

My folks had compassion which sprang from their own place of having lived with unmet needs. Both were reared in needy and struggling families. For Christmas, our family always had a live tree that dad would spray paint white to make it look snow covered. It was our family tradition. Dad would buy the tree and take it to his shop where he would spray it and let it dry. He brought it home on the day we were to decorate it. As kids, we loved watching him drive up in his pickup truck with that tree in the back. One tree-trimming day arrived, but when Dad came home, there was a beautiful green tree in the truck instead of a white one. When we questioned him about our traditional tree, he told us this story. As he was at his warehouse loading up our white tree to bring home, a little boy came up to him and said, "Mister, that's the most beautiful Christmas tree I've ever seen." Dad asked him what kind of Christmas tree he had, to which he replied, his family couldn't afford a tree. Dad drove the little boy to his home and carried the tree into his house. That year we were proud to have a green tree and also very proud of our dad.

There was a blind lady who lived a few houses from our church. Mom and I would visit her every week. I played with her granddaughter while Mom did some practical things to help her. Mom was always quick to prepare a meal or give money when someone had a special need. These memories would be more connecting dots to WLFJ. My parents instilled into us care and compassion for others by their beautiful example. My sister, Susan, worked in the kitchen of a nursing home for some time. She always looked for ways to bless those she served with little extras that would bring a bit of joy into their lives. My brother is a very generous business man and has a heart to bless others. God has used our parents, even with their great brokenness, to cultivate compassion for others in us.

My parents moved away from the rural area where they were raised and started a new life for themselves. However, they brought with them the bondage from their heritage. My mom decided to go to business school when I was a baby. They rented a small apartment in a large house. Their neighbors in that house were a couple much older than them with their own set of problems. This was the lady's second marriage and her children from her first marriage were being raised in an orphanage. The man was a prison guard and an alcoholic. They struggled with life, but befriended this young family that moved in across the hall from them. When Mom went to school and then later to work, it seemed to be the perfect solution to have the Pointers, living right next door, care for me. It was convenient, they were friendly, and they needed the money. I have a little video that plays in my memory. As a young child, I was sitting on the floor playing while Dad and Mr. Pointer were enjoying a drink together, laughing and talking. Mr. Pointer was one of the men from my childhood that I had to forgive.

My parents were blind to the unhealthy lifestyle of the Pointers. When I was a toddler, I broke my collarbone while in their care. They told my parents that I rolled off the bed. My parents never questioned the accident. In Mom and Dad's eyes, they could do no wrong. By the time my sister and brother came along, Mom was staying at home to raise her three children, and they never were involved much with the Pointers. I can remember Mr. Pointer calling my dad and crying because he wanted to see me, and Dad would make me go visit. Mr. Pointer had an unhealthy, unnatural desire to see me. Years later, as a young adult and working, I would see him sometimes when I walked downtown on my lunch break. I always crossed the street to the other side so he never saw me. My parents would often tell me how much the Pointers loved me and that I should go visit them. I had no desire to see either of them. It was many years later before I understood this strange relationship and my odd feelings toward them.

Many of the young ladies who have been in my life and that I've had the great privilege of knowing and encouraging could fit easily into my life story. Their stories were similar. Many were much worse. As I looked into the faces of the ladies in the prison Bible Study, I saw sisters who had not received the help that I had received. I longed for them to know how much Jesus loved them and how their stories could be redeemed. It was part of my stewardship for all that Jesus has given me to gladly be passed along. My counselor, Debbie, was a young mother when she helped me and had only a small amount of time to invest in others. Her prayer was that those she was able to help would be people who would pass it on to others. In many ways, I not only benefited by her investment in me, but also her prayer. I have had the great privilege to pass it on. Some of the ladies from the prison class came to live with us, but most only came to Wednesday night Bible Study at the prison. A few others also qualified to go on outings with our team to church, to our homes for a few hours, or out for a shopping day. The cry of my heart was for them to get discipleship, healing, and equipping while in prison so that once they were released, they could truly enjoy a new life in the world outside of the prison gates. I loved watching them become free in prison and enjoy their new life in Christ before they ever experienced physical freedom. There were always some that floated in and out of class but never truly benefited.

I did not have to look far to find someone that did not benefit. My younger sister was abused as a child in a situation totally different from mine. I had the privilege of leading her to the Lord when she was a young mother struggling with life. I loved her and wanted to see her break out into her own freedom. There were times when her heart opened, but then suddenly, she closed down. As time passed, the little windows of willingness to reach outside her bondage became smaller and smaller. Her life only became harder with each year. She was unhappy much of the time. Bitterness, anger, frustration, and resentment seemed to become her constant companions. She had few friends and never really knew what it was like to enjoy a church family. We talked regularly and sometimes she allowed me to pray with her. She loved her three children and tried hard to be a good mother. Even in her brokenness, she sowed much good into the lives of her children that continues to reap a harvest. My brother and I tried to help her. He offered to pay for her to get counseling, but she refused.

I am struck by how people who have experienced similar situations can respond so differently to them. Some are always victims. Others become victorious. We have no choice about the family we are born into or many of the situations of our lives, but we have a choice about what we do with the experiences that come our way. I have seen ladies who have suffered huge destruction grab ahold of God and not give up until they received back from Him double blessings for all their pain. I know that God is blessed and happy when we take Him at His Word and receive all He has for us. One of these ladies is my dear friend, Sally.

I met Sally the first day I visited the prison. She started her prison sentence on death row, but when I met her, she was serving a life sentence. Sally had taken her husband's life. She would be the first to tell you today that she was wrong in how she responded to life's circumstances. Sally came from a broken heritage as well and married a man that badly abused her. She had a son from a previous marriage and was constantly concerned for his welfare. Forty-five years ago, the help that we have today for battered women did not exist. Sally was a hard worker and tried to rise above the circumstances of her life, but she did not know the Lord at the time. The final straw for Sally came when her husband beat her so badly that she had a miscarriage causing the baby she was carrying to die. Eventually, she poisoned her husband in order to break free from this abusive situation for herself and her son. Sally was incarcerated and soon thereafter came to know the Lord. She was a well-educated lady, a school teacher before prison. When I met Sally, she had been in prison for several years. Because of her crime she could not qualify for work release, but was able to go to school. She did everything she could to better herself while incarcerated.

I enjoyed watching Sally grow in the Lord. She was quick to do anything she could for others. Her heart was tender toward inmates and officers. She altered uniforms for many of the prison guards. She taught ladies in prison to read and to make things so they could have gifts to give their children when they visited. She was a friend to anyone who wanted a friend and she brought many ladies to Bible Study. I went to the superintendent to see what could be done for Sally. She told me Sally would never leave prison. But Sally had a word from the Lord that she was going to be released. Each time a parole hearing came up, I would go to speak on her behalf. Time passed, but Sally would not give up. In time she earned the privilege of home passes and would go home once or twice a month and spend the weekend with her sister. As God would have it, her sister's neighbor was the daughter of a man that Sally had known in high school. They had even dated for a while. His wife had died from cancer a few years earlier. They became friends again and, in a few years, he asked her to marry him. Sam and I were honored to be invited to their wedding at the prison. Sally was now able to go home for visits with her husband. When another parole hearing came up, her husband, her son, and I went to ask the parole board for Sally's release. After more than 20 years, it was granted to her. Sally's life is a beautiful story of redemption. She dared to believe God and she dared to grab hold of His hand. She dared to enjoy her life in prison as she expectantly awaited God's redemption and the fulfillment of His promise. It has been my privilege to know Sally and others like her who have chosen to trust God in life's difficult circumstances.

I look into the faces of people every week who have suffered abuse, or have generational poverty, or have other great bondage. It is a privilege to watch the beautiful, amazing Body of Christ come to WLFJ to serve and love their neighbors. Seeds are planted. Hope is shared. Lives are changed. Our hope becomes the fuel for someone else to have hope.

Hope is not just a word. Hope is not something we want to see happen. Hope is action. Hope becomes reality through revelation from God. Hope means we walk in expectancy, anticipation, assurance, confidence, and a watchful eye for God to show up, work and do exactly what He has promised. He says that He will never leave me alone. My response to that truth is to walk it in hope. My part is to walk confidently revealing by my actions that I am NOT alone. God is teaching me to 'rejoice in hope.' How I live my life displays what I believe! God has called us, His children, to walk daily before Him rejoicing in the reality of what He has said as though we see it already. We see it with the eye of faith. We are called to walk in expectancy.

When God speaks to us or promises us something, the next step is ours. That step is called hope. With our eyes focused securely on Jesus, the One who spoke, we begin to live it. My friend Sally didn't simply wish that she would one day get out of prison. Based on what God said, she began to live it. She looked at her days in that prison as limited and needed them to count for eternity, so she witnessed to others and served others well. Sally made plans with her husband for things they would do on her upcoming release. When the circumstances of life seemed overwhelming, she learned to talk to herself with the truth. Together, we would say, "The fact is another parole was turned down. But, the **truth** is God has said release is coming." She needed to be ready. It's not a mind over matter mentality. It's a **truth** over facts way of life. We are called to face the facts and then walk in the truth of what God has said. Abraham looked at his body and faced the facts that he and Sarah could not have children. Then, he chose to believe God and lived in that expectancy.

We study and study the Word of God. Study is good. However, study without application becomes only knowledge that can cause us to be proud about having the answers. The Word warns that knowledge can puff up. To know truth and not walk truth can be dangerous. What was meant to bring freedom can actually bring hardness of heart. Hope is not only to be studied. It is to be lived! It also becomes contagious!

The second man I would need to forgive from my childhood was a Sunday school teacher and youth leader. He, too, was a friend of my parents. He also took an unusual interest in me. I found out later that I was one of several whom he hurt. When the Lord pulled back the veil and allowed me to see those situations, it was like a video playing in my mind. I could see the brick wall I was walking on with Mr. Pointer holding my hand, and the details were vivid. In this situation with Mr. Knight, the Sunday school teacher, it was much the same. There were specific incidents that God showed me. One of those was at the beach with my youth group. I could clearly see the strand of the beach and even feel the night air. The thing that always puzzled me was that the beach looked different from any beach I had ever seen in our area. Because of that, the enemy would try to make me think I had made it up. I would quickly take that thought captive, but it kept coming back. One day, God settled that for me.

My friend, Don, heads up a ministry that serves ministry leaders. For several years, he put together a ministry getaway for leaders at a Christian facility. I attended the prayer retreat for the first time many years after I had dealt with the abuse and was already walking in great freedom. I unloaded my things from the car and headed to get a quick walk on the beach before we gathered for our first prayer time together. As I stepped onto the beach alone with Jesus and began to walk and talk with Him, I realized this beach looked familiar. I continued to walk and rounded an area that looked all too familiar. It was from the video in my mind. There is a section of the beach that has a stone wall. When the tide comes in, it comes to that wall. In my video, I was trapped between that wall and the incoming tide and could not get away from Mr. Knight. I stood in disbelief as I saw this beach again for the first time after more than twenty-five years. The Lord's mercy and compassion to me was amazing. There was no pain as I looked at this place. The pain had been dealt with, but there would be no more taunts from the enemy now that I had seen it.

Several years after this prayer retreat, Troy and his family joined the WLFJ family, and he took the role of Director of Outreach. He was new at the ministry and another prayer retreat was coming up. Troy was invited to attend as well. He and I traveled together to the retreat and had a great time of getting to know each other better. In the years between my initial trip and this one, I always walked that beach once during my stay, but God had shown me a getaway place to go while there to spend special time with Him. I would not allow that beach to be fearful for me. I always took one walk, but I could not wait to get to the place God set aside for us. On this particular trip, it rained nearly all the time. I did not get my usual walk on the beach as a result. Every day of the retreat, Troy asked me if I had walked the beach. Finally, he told me there was something on the beach he wanted me to see. I assured him I'd walk it before I left. The days got away and it was our last morning there and the group of ministry leaders had assembled for our last prayer time before heading home. Once it was over, we were on a tight time schedule. Troy again asked me if I had walked the beach. I felt bad that I had forgotten to make this a priority as I had promised. We slipped out of the meeting and headed to the beach in the pouring rain. We both got soaked. I felt silly but trusted God that there was a good reason for this. Troy led me to the very spot from my video and on the sand dune was a huge heart drawn in the sand. On the inside of the heart were the words, "Sam loves you." I was overcome by the presence and sweetness of the Lord. Troy knew nothing about this beach or my past. It had rained on and off for days. Troy drew the heart the first day we arrived and in all that rain, it had not washed away. How precious of the Lord to replace that old video with such a beautiful picture. Troy was right. Sam does love me. Though he'd be the first to tell you he is not perfect, he is the perfect husband for me and dealt well with the unearthing of my painful past and the healing process. Sam later shook Troy's hand and thanked him for that sweet message written on the beach on his behalf.

When God first revealed my past to me, my first response

was, "what is wrong with me." I realized after reading Buhler's book, that there are wicked people in this world who can spot those who are likely prey. They can see places where needs have not been met in a child's life, and use that to victimize them. I was one of those children. There was nothing wrong with me, I was their victim. However, I did not stay a victim. What the enemy meant for harm and destruction, God has taken and used for honor and blessing in my life as well as the lives of others.

One morning as I was sitting with Jesus and watching the sun break through the darkness, my heart was filled to overflowing with gratitude to Him for how He stepped into my life. He stepped into my darkness and brought His amazing light. Tears flowed freely as I fought to find words to express my thanks for all that God has done for me and for our family. I looked squarely at the destruction of my life—my family, my heritage, my own many bad choices—and could not even allow myself to wonder or begin to visualize what would have happened to me, to us, without His intervention. "Thank you Lord Jesus!"

It is interesting to look back to see that one prison guard and one Sunday school teacher would be tools of the enemy in my life. However, God gave me the beautiful opportunity to serve for more than twenty years in the prison. I had many opportunities to befriend and minister to some of the officers and staff as well as residents during that time. There were many prison guards whom I came to respect and many that God allowed me to help. I have also been given the great privilege of encouraging many churches and many godly Sunday school teachers to serve together at WLFJ to display our amazing and beautiful unity. God's ways are certainly beyond our ways. His ways are always right and good! Satan appointed one prison guard and one deceived Sunday school teacher to do his bidding. But, God in His redemption of my past has given me many more opportunities to bless prison guards and Sunday school teachers and to be blessed by them.

It is true that I hate the brokenness and pain that came out of my childhood. However, this is also true: I would not trade having walked this road for anything. The Lord has more than healed, and redeemed, and set me free. He has used it as an investment in His Kingdom. The results will be enjoyed throughout all eternity! I am blessed beyond words!

As I serve at WLFJ with many brothers and sisters in Christ, and especially as I look at the wonderful team of leaders that God has given me to serve with there, I am awestruck by the truth that it's out of their own pain and brokenness that God does great work. I have watched volunteers who have lost their jobs, suffered great illness, or have huge pain in their personal lives and families, set those things aside to come and serve together. They have faced the truth that they can do nothing to change their own situation. Yet they have given it over to God, rolled up their sleeves, and gotten busy in God's Kingdom work. As they do this, they have seen God work in their own places of hurt and pain in incredible ways.

One of my earliest memories from the prison is one that continues to stick in my mind. It was an unusual inmate who admitted she was in prison because of their own wrong. It seems that everybody (in and out of prison) blames someone else for their wrong. It didn't surprise me when one day Marcie told me she was incarcerated because she had been wrongly accused of killing someone. Her husband was a pastor and had committed adultery, and the young woman involved had a baby. Marcie became aware of her husband's sin as well as this baby which the mother did not want. She not only forgave her husband, but also took this child to rear as her own. A couple of years later, this little child died at the hands of someone. Marcie was accused, declared guilty, and went to prison. Marcie had several children of her own. I could not get past the fact that she was different from most inmates who declared their innocence. She told me one day that God knew exactly where she was, and she was going to roll up her sleeves and get busy until He freed her. She did just that. She shared the Word and she encouraged others. She was available to God for however He wanted to use her in prison. One Saturday morning, I opened the paper to see Marcie's picture on the front page of it. Her little children were lined up outside the prison fence with their faces pressed against it, watching their mom pulling a wagon containing all her prison possessions, headed for the gate to be released. The headlines read, "Mom found not guilty." Marcie will always be a hero to me. Bad things do happen to good people. God's people roll up their sleeves and ask Him to redeem and use it!

Sally, Marcie, and so many others have faced their brokenness, their abuse, their wrongs, and have dared to believe that their God was bigger. They've dared to believe that God could redeem, restore, and use them and their pain. Their God is big enough, great enough, to use even them. Many people spend a lifetime going to counselors, reading books, and talking about their pain instead of taking the next step of obedience and watching God show up. Being broken doesn't keep God from using us, but it often is used by the enemy to make us feel unusable. When we cower in fear and refuse to obey God's direction because we think He can't use us, we are not limiting ourselves, but we are limiting our God!

* * *

Now, you have heard the story of God's redemption and faithfulness to me and my family as we have walked and continue to walk our unseen path with God. What does this have to do with where you and I are today in our lives on planet earth? How does God want to use us, even in our continued brokenness and healing, in His unfolding plan to build His Kingdom on earth as it is in Heaven?

When I look at the beautiful way God has stepped into brokenness in my life, and into the lives of my brothers and sisters in Christ, to accomplish His great purposes, it gives me much hope for America. The truth is that much of our brokenness comes from our own sin and failures. That does not keep Redeemer God, Restorer God, and Almighty God from being able to use them to accomplish His purposes. We repent, we cry out to Him to forgive and redeem, and He does! I've watched us as Americans make huge mistakes and commit unbelievable sins against our wonderful God. We have taken prayer out of school, made it legal to kill pre-born babies, and the list continues. Our sin is great.

I watch on the news the latest accounts of militant groups, deranged minds, and catastrophes which make my heart ache with the devastation in our nation and the world around us. Yet, we seem blind to the mass devastation around us. Through abortions, we have greatly devalued life by condoning the killing of pre-born babies, and then we question why life seems to have no value any more. If we can justify killing an innocent pre-born baby, how do we expect our youth to think that taking a born life is any different? God forgive us! Our conversations are filled with exclamations of horror over what we've seen on the news. We criticize and label others, but we overlook our own guilt!

In the founding years of our nation, believers were not afraid of other religions or sects. Our forefathers walked an incredible standard based on the Word of God. They knew their influence would win those of others religions over to Christ. They lived "light." Their walks were "salty." Over the years as our devotion and love for Jesus has waned, our nation became vulnerable to those other false teachings. Our open-mindedness replaced our resolve. Compromise became popular. We have become influenced instead of influencing. Walls of integrity and truth have come down causing us to lose standards set by God for our protection. Instead we've built walls within the Body of Christ and somehow justified our behavior as having to protect ourselves from other believers. What a mess! Yet even this mess is not too hard for our God!

This is our time in what will soon be called history. We have been appointed to this time. My brokenness cannot become my excuse for not allowing God to use me to accomplish His purposes. God easily uses broken people. He is not weakened by our lack. He is all powerful, amazing God and His ability infuses our inability and history is changed.

The Body of Christ must step outside our local churches and join together to display our unity so that we shine brighter and our saltiness becomes more productive. There are lots of places where we can do this. WLFJ is one of those places and this is what we have been called to do—to display unity—to shine Jesus—to be salty together—to show the dying world around us that we love and belong to Jesus by loving each other. We have to tear down the walls we've allowed our enemy to convince us are necessary. This is a little step, but this little step empowered by our great God can do more than we can imagine!

God was willing to save Sodom and Gomorrah for the sake of ten righteous ones. We focus on the fact that God destroyed those cities. Yet, for the sake of ten, He would have held back judgment. The problem was that there were not ten righteous ones to be found. Our focus is often on the sin in America. Yet God's focus is the godly, on the righteous, on those who are crying out in repentance hoping to be another voice that will make a difference. Lot did not use his influence for good. Instead he was influenced by evil. Yes, America deserves destruction. Our sin is great, but the influence of His righteous children is greater. Our God is merciful and nothing is too difficult for Him. If He would have spared Sodom and Gomorrah for the sake of ten, how might He restore and redeem America because of the cry of His righteous children. Maybe just one more believer confessing his or her sin and getting right with God and choosing to walk righteously before Him will make the difference!

Nineveh was on the path to be destroyed. Yet one man's preaching was used by God to turn the entire city to Him and judgment was stayed. I'm struck by the words of a wicked king in Jonah 3:9: *Who knows? God may yet relent and with compassion turn from his fierce anger so that we will not perish.* As I continue to read in Jonah 4:11: *But Nineveh has more than a hundred and twenty thousand people who cannot tell their right hand from their left, and many cattle as well. Should I not be concerned about that great city?* I am moved by the truth seen in these verses. God's compassion overtook His fierce anger.

God may choose to be merciful to us. He will restore His Body as we confess and forsake our sin. Our future doesn't rest in the political arena. It rests in His people who are called, who are willing to make things right with Him, and then be used by Him. He could give America another chance to be used to touch the world. I believe the day can come when the world around us could stand amazed at all that America's God has done to redeem her huge sin. He will be gloried—not America! The generations to follow us would be able to say that because of this generation's restoration, blessings will fall on them for a thousand generations! "So be it, Lord God!"

He Is Working
By Jim Meadows

The hurting and the hungry come
Seeking help and find the Son
A ministry of life and love is here
The power of a spirit birth
The blessing of a life that's turned
The wonder of his grace can bring out tears

Chorus
He is working in this place
Helping guests and volunteers
Hearing every humble prayer
Never seen but always here
He is working with the weary
Giving rest for broken lives
Showing them his yoke is easy
And his burden is so light
He is working...

Jesus walks upon these floors
Touching lives forevermore
Building souls and healing bodies too
Serving hands are joined with His
Teaching every one to give
This ministry declares His words of truth

Every gift is from above
Signed with perfect cleansing blood
All **with love from Jesus**
All **with love from Jesus**

He is working...always working

ACKNOWLEDGEMENTS

I would like to thank Jesus for calling me to walk His Path, and then allowing me to write about it. It has been, and continues to be, an amazing journey. I marvel at His great love for His children.

I am thankful to Sam for being man enough not to feel threatened by this woman that God has given him to walk with on Planet Earth. He has often been the voice of reason, or the reminder to me, of what God has said to us.

I would like to thank my family for loving me unconditionally. I know this was said in the dedication, but it cannot be said enough. Each one means more to me than any words could express. I am blessed!

I want to thank the many volunteers at With Love From Jesus who pour their lives into this ministry and quickly get on board with what God is doing among us. They understand "unity."

I am thankful to Amanda Gawthorpe for continuing to be my friend after editing this book. She has accepted it as a labor of love for Jesus!

I would like to thank Blue Ink Press for trusting God enough to give me the chance to publish this book with them. It is a wonderful partnership and a great adventure for me.

Made in the USA
San Bernardino, CA
03 August 2018